making classroom
ASSESSMENTS

reliable & valid

robert j. marzano

Solution Tree | Press

a division of
Solution Tree

555 North Morton Street
Bloomington, IN 47404
800.733.6786 (toll free) / 812.336.7700
FAX: 812.336.7790

email: info@SolutionTree.com
SolutionTree.com

Visit **go.SolutionTree.com/assessment** to download the free reproducibles in this book.

Printed in the United States of America

21   20   19   18   17   1   2   3   4   5

Names: Marzano, Robert J., author.

Title: Making classroom assessments reliable and valid / Robert J. Marzano.

Description: Bloomington, IN : Solution Tree Press, [2018] | Includes
   bibliographical references and index.

Identifiers: LCCN 2017011403 | ISBN 9781945349171 (perfect bound)

Subjects: LCSH: Educational tests and measurements--United States. | Grading
   and marking (Students)--United States.

Classification: LCC LB3051 .M4577 2018 | DDC 371.260973--dc23 LC record available at https://lccn.loc.gov/2017011403

Solution Tree
Jeffrey C. Jones, CEO
Edmund M. Ackerman, President

Solution Tree Press
President and Publisher: Douglas M. Rife
Editorial Director: Sarah Payne-Mills
Managing Production Editor: Caroline Cascio
Senior Editor: Amy Rubenstein
Proofreader: Miranda Addonizio
Text and Cover Designer: Abigail Bowen
Editorial Assistants: Jessi Finn and Kendra Slayton

Table of Contents

About the Author vii

Introduction
THE ROLE OF CLASSROOM ASSESSMENT 1
The Curious History of Large-Scale Assessments 2

The Place of Classroom Assessment 6

Reliability and Validity at the Heart of the Matter 7

The Need for New Paradigms 8

The Large-Scale Assessment Paradigm for Reliability 8

    The Equation for a Single Score 10

    The Reliability Coefficient 10

The New CA Paradigm for Reliability 11

The Large-Scale Assessment Paradigm for Validity 13

The New CA Paradigm for Validity 14

What to Expect in This Book 15

Chapter 1
DISCUSSING THE CLASSROOM ASSESSMENT PARADIGM FOR VALIDITY 17
The Instrumental Perspective 18

The Argument-Based Perspective 20

Standards as the Basis of CA Validity 21

    The Standards Movement 21

    The Problem With Standards 21

Dimensionality 22

Measurement Topics and Proficiency Scales 25

The Rise of Learning Progressions. 25

The Structure of Proficiency Scales. 28

The School's Role in Criterion-Related Validity 32

The Nature of Parallel Assessments. 33

The Measurement Process 34

Summary 37

Chapter 2
DESIGNING AND SCORING
PARALLEL ASSESSMENTS 39

Traditional Tests. 39

    Designing Selected-Response Items 40

    Designing Short Constructed-Response Items. 42

    Scoring Assessments That Use Selected-Response and Short
    Constructed-Response Items 43

Essays 47

Performance Tasks, Demonstrations, and Presentations 48

Portfolios. 50

Probing Discussions. 51

Student Self-Assessments. 52

Assessments That Cover One Level of a
  Proficiency Scale. 55

    Voting Techniques. 55

    Observations 55

    Student-Generated Assessments 56

The Complete Measurement Process. 56

Assessment Planning. 56

Differentiated Assessments 58

Summary 58

Chapter 3
DISCUSSING THE CA PARADIGM FOR RELIABILITY..59

Discussing the Traditional View of Reliability. .59

    Foundations of the Traditional Concept of Reliability 60

    The Concept of Error Score 60

    The Concept of True Score 61

    The Correlation Coefficient and the Reliability Coefficient. 61

    The Conceptual Formula for Reliability 63

    The Reliability Determination Using a Single Test 63

The Achilles Heel of the Reliability Coefficient 64

Estimating True Scores Using Mathematical Models 65

    The Linear Trend Line 66

    The Curvilinear Trend Line 67

    The Average Trend Line 67

    Model Reconciliation 68

    Model of Best Fit 68

Using Technology 70

Discussing the Implications for Formative and Summative Scores 72

Using Instructional Feedback 73

Employing the Method of Mounting Evidence 74

Considering the Issue of Scales 76

    Proficiency Scales as Inherently Ordinal .79

    Proficiency Scales That Are Internally Consistent 80

    The Strong Statistics Theory 81

Summary 81

Chapter 4
MEASURING GROWTH FOR GROUPS OF STUDENTS.. 83

Measuring Growth 84

    Linear Growth Score 84

    The Curvilinear Growth Score 86

    The Difference Score 88

Reconciling the Three Reliabilities 90

Using Technology to Help Teachers 91

Summary 92

Chapter 5
TRANSFORMING THE SYSTEM USING THE NEW CLASSROOM ASSESSMENT PARADIGMS 93

Transforming Report Cards 93

    Weighted and Unweighted Averages 99

    The Median and the Mode 102

    The Conjunctive Approach 102

    A Supplemental Measurement Topic 104

    The Practice of Allowing Students to Increase Their Scores 105

Transforming Teacher Evaluations 106

Summary 108

Appendix
TECHNICAL NOTES 109

Technical Note 1.1: Confidence Intervals 110

Technical Note 3.1: Linear Trend Line 111

Technical Note 3.2: Curvilinear Trend Line 112

Technical Note 3.3: Trend Line for the Average.......................... 114

Technical Note 3.4: The Method of Mounting Evidence 115

Technical Note 4.1: Reliability of Linear Growth Scores 118

Technical Note 4.2: Reliability of Curvilinear Growth Scores.......... 120

Technical Note 4.3: Reliability of Difference Scores 121

References and Resources......................... 123

Index 133

About the Author

Robert J. Marzano, PhD, is the cofounder and chief academic officer of Marzano Research in Denver, Colorado. During his fifty years in the field of education, he has worked with educators as a speaker and trainer and has authored more than forty books and three hundred articles on topics such as instruction, assessment, writing and implementing standards, cognition, effective leadership, and school intervention. His books include *The New Art and Science of Teaching, Leaders of Learning, The Classroom Strategies Series, A Handbook for High Reliability Schools, Awaken the Learner,* and *Managing the Inner World of Teaching.* His practical translations of the most current research and theory into classroom strategies are known internationally and are widely practiced by both teachers and administrators.

He received a bachelor's degree from Iona College in New York, a master's degree from Seattle University, and a doctorate from the University of Washington.

To learn more about Robert J. Marzano's work, visit marzanoresearch.com.

To book Robert J. Marzano for professional development, contact pd@SolutionTree.com.

The Role of Classroom Assessment

Classroom assessment has been largely ignored in the research and practice of assessment theory. This is not to say that it has been inconsequential to classroom practice. To the contrary, the topic of classroom assessment has become more and more popular in the practitioner literature. For example, the book *Classroom Assessment: What Teachers Need to Know* is in its eighth edition (Popham, 2017). Many other publishers continue to release books on the topic. This trend notwithstanding, technical literature in the 20th century has rarely mentioned classroom assessment. As James McMillan (2013b) notes:

> Throughout most of the 20th century, the research on assessment in education focused on the role of standardized testing . . . . It was clear that the professional educational measurement community was concerned with the role of standardized testing, both from a large-scale assessment perspective as well as with how teachers used test data for instruction in their own classrooms. (p. 4)

As evidence, McMillan (2013b) notes that an entire issue of the *Journal of Educational Measurement* that purported to focus on state-of-the-art testing and instruction did not address teacher-made tests. Additionally, the first three editions of *Educational Measurement* (Lindquist, 1951; Linn, 1993; Thorndike, 1971)—which are designed to summarize the state of the art in measurement research, theory, and practice—paid little if any attention to classroom assessment. Finally, both editions of *The Standards for Educational and Psychological Testing* (American Educational Research Association [AERA], American Psychological Association [APA], & National Council on Measurement in Education [NCME], 1999, 2014)—which, as their titles indicate, are designed to set standards for testing in both psychology and education—made little explicit reference to classroom assessment. It wasn't until the fourth edition in the first decade of the 21st century (Brennan, 2006) that a chapter was included addressing classroom assessment.

Most recently, the *SAGE Handbook of Research on Classroom Assessment* made a stand for the rightful place of classroom assessment: "This book is based on a single assertion: Classroom assessment (CA) is the most powerful type of measurement in education that influences student learning" (McMillan,

2013a, p. xxiii). Throughout this text, I take the same perspective. I also use the convention of referring to classroom assessment as CA. Since the publication of the *SAGE Handbook*, this abbreviation is now the norm in many technical discussions of classroom assessment theory. My intent is for this book to be both technical and practical.

What, then, is the place of CAs in the current K–12 system of assessment, and what is their future? This resource attempts to lay out a future for CA that will render it the primary source of evidence regarding student learning; this would stand in stark contrast to the current situation in which formal measurements of students are left to interim assessments, end-of-course assessments, and state assessments. In this introduction, I will discuss several topics with regard to CAs.

- The curious history of large-scale assessments
- The place of classroom assessment
- Reliability and validity at the heart of the matter
- The need for new paradigms
- The large-scale assessment paradigm for reliability
- The new CA paradigm for reliability
- The large-scale assessment paradigm for validity
- The new CA paradigm for validity

Before delving directly into the future of CA, it is useful to consider the general history of large-scale assessments in U.S. education since it is the foundation of current practices in CA.

The Curious History of Large-Scale Assessments

The present and future of CA are intimately tied to the past and present of large-scale assessments. In 2001, educational measurement expert Robert Linn published "A Century of Standardized Testing: Controversies and Pendulum Swings." Linn notes that the original purpose of large-scale assessment was comparison and began in the 19th century.

Educators commonly refer to J. M. Rice as the inventor of the comparative large-scale assessment. This assignment is based on his 1895 assessment of the spelling ability of some thirty-three thousand students in grades 4 through 12 for which comparative results were reported (Engelhart & Thomas, 1966). However, assessments that educators administered to several hundred students in seventeen schools in Boston and one school in Roxbury in 1845 predated this comparative large-scale assessment. Because of this, Horace Mann (who initiated the effort) deserves credit as the first to administer large-scale tests. Lorrie A. Shepard (2008) elaborates on the contribution of Horace Mann, noting:

> In 1845, Massachusetts State Superintendent of Instruction, Horace Mann, pressured Boston school trustees to adopt written examinations because large increases in enrollments made oral exams unfeasible. Long

before IQ tests, these examinations were used to classify pupils . . . and to put comparative information about how schools were doing in the hands of state-level authority. (p. 25)

Educators designed these early large-scale assessments to help solve perceived problems within the K–12 system. For example, in 1909, Leonard P. Ayres published the book *Laggards in Our Schools: A Study of Retardation and Elimination in City School Systems*. Despite the book's lack of sensitivity to labeling large groups of students in unflattering ways, it brought attention to the problems associated with repeated retention of students in grade levels. This helped buttress the goal of reformers who wanted to develop programs that would mitigate failure.

The first half of the 20th century was not a flattering era for large-scale assessments. They focused on natural intelligence, and educators used them to classify examinees. To say the least, this era did not represent the initial or current intent of large-scale assessment. I address this period in more detail shortly.

By the second half of the 20th century, educators began to use large-scale assessments more effectively. Such assessments were a central component of James Bryant Conant's (1953) vision of schools designed to provide students with guidance as to appropriate career paths and support in realizing related careers.

The use of large-scale assessment increased dramatically in the 1960s. According to Shepard (2008), the modern era of large-scale assessment started in the mid-1960s: "Title I of the Elementary and Secondary Education Act (ESEA) of 1965 launched the development of the field of educational evaluation and the school accountability movement" (p. 26). Shepard (2008) explains that it was the ESEA mandate for data with which to scrutinize the reform efforts that compelled the research community to develop more finely tuned evaluation tools: "The American Educational Research Association began a monograph series in 1967 to disseminate the latest thinking in evaluation theory, and several educational evaluation organizations and journals date from this period" (p. 26).

The National Assessment of Educational Progress (NAEP) began in 1969 and "was part of the same general trend toward large-scale data gathering" (Shepard, 2008, p. 27). However, researchers and policymakers designed NAEP for program evaluation as opposed to individual student performance evaluation.

The need to gather and utilize data about individual students started minimum competency testing in the United States. This spread quickly, and by 1980 "all states had a minimum competency testing program or a state testing program of some kind" (Shepard, 2008, p. 31). But this, too, ran aground because of the amount of time and resources necessary for large-scale competency tests.

The next wave of school reform was the "excellence movement" spawned by the high visibility report *A Nation at Risk* (National Commission on Excellence in Education, 1983). It cited low standards and a watered-down curriculum as reasons for the lackluster performance of U.S. schools. It also faulted the minimum competency movement, noting that focusing on minimum requirements distracted educators from the more noble and appropriate goal of maximizing students' competencies.

Fueled by these criticisms, researchers and policymakers focused on the identification of rigorous and challenging standards for all students in the core subject areas. Standards work in mathematics set the tone for the reform:

> Leading the way, the National Council of Teachers of Mathematics report on *Curriculum and Evaluation Standards for School Mathematics* (1989) expanded the purview of elementary school mathematics to include geometry and spatial sense, measurement, statistics and probability, and patterns and relationships, and at the same time emphasized problem solving, communication, mathematical reasoning, and mathematical connections rather than computation and rote activities. (Shepard, 2008, p. 35)

By the early 1990s, virtually every major academic subject area had sample standards for K–12 education.

Shepard (2008) notes that standards-based reform, begun in the 1990s, "is the most enduring of test-based accountability reforms" (p. 37). However, she also cautioned that the version of this reform enacted in No Child Left Behind (NCLB) "contradicts core principles of the standards movement" mostly because the assessments associated with NCLB did not place ample focus on the application and use of knowledge reflected in the standards researchers developed (Shepard, 2008, p. 37). Also, the accountability system that accompanied NCLB focused on rewards and punishments.

The beginning of the new century saw an emphasis on testing that was highly focused on standards. In 2009, the National Governors Association Center for Best Practices (NGA) and the Council of Chief State School Officers (CCSSO) partnered in "a state-led process that [drew] evidence and [led] to development and adoption of a common core of state standards . . . in English language arts and mathematics for grades K–12" (as cited in Rothman, 2011, p. 62). This effort, referred to as the *Common Core State Standards (CCSS)*, resulted in the establishment of two state consortia that were tasked with designing new assessments aligned to the standards. One consortium was the Partnership for Assessment of Readiness for College and Careers (PARCC); the other was the Smarter Balanced Assessment Consortium (SBAC):

> Each consortium planned to offer several different kinds of assessments aligned to the CCSS, including year-end summative assessments, interim or benchmark assessments (used throughout the school year), and resources that teachers could use for formative assessment in the classroom. In addition to being computer-administered, these new assessments would include performance tasks, which require students to demonstrate a skill or procedure or create a product. (Marzano, Yanoski, Hoegh, & Simms, 2013, p. 7)

These efforts are still under way although with less widespread use than in their initiation.

Next, I discuss previous abuses of large-scale assessments that occurred in the first half of the 20th century (Houts, 1977). To illustrate the nature and extent of these abuses, consider the first intelligence test usable for groups that Alfred Binet developed in 1905. It was grounded in the theory that intelligence was not a fixed entity. Rather, educators could remediate low intelligence if they identified it. As Leon J. Kamin (1977) notes in his book on the nature and use of his IQ test, Binet includes a chapter, "The Training of Intelligence," in which he outlines educational interventions for those who scored low on his test. There was clearly an implied focus on helping low-performing students. It wasn't until the Americanized version of the Stanford-Binet test (by Lewis M. Terman, 1916) that the concept of IQ solidified as a fixed entity with little or no chance of improvement. Consequently, educators would use the IQ test to identify students with low intelligence so they could monitor and deal with them accordingly. Terman (1916) notes:

> In the near future intelligence tests will bring tens of thousands of these high-grade defectives under the surveillance and protection of society. This will ultimately result in curtailing the reproduction of feeble-mindedness and in the elimination of an enormous amount of crime, pauperism, and industrial inefficiency. It is hardly necessary to emphasize that the high-grade cases, of the type now so frequently overlooked, are precisely the ones whose guardianship it is most important for the State to assume. (pp. 6-7)

The perspective that Lewis Terman articulated became widespread in the United States and led to the development of Arthur Otis's (one of Terman's students) Army Alpha test. According to Kamin (1977), performance scores for 125,000 draftees were analyzed and published in 1921 by the National Academy of Sciences, titled *Memoirs of the National Academy of Sciences: Psychological Examining in the United States Army* (Yerkes, 1921). The report contains the chapter "Relation of Intelligence Ratings to Nativity," which focuses on an analysis of about twelve thousand draftees who reported that they were born outside of the United States. Educators assigned a letter grade from A to E for each of the draftees, and the distribution of these letter grades was analyzed for each country. The report notes:

> The range of differences between the countries is a very wide one . . . . In general, the Scandinavian and English speaking countries stand high in the list, while the Slavic and Latin countries stand low . . . the countries tend to fall into two groups: Canada, Great Britain, the Scandinavian and Teutonic countries . . . [as opposed to] the Latin and Slavic countries. (Yerkes, 1921, p. 699)

Clearly, the perspective regarding intelligence has changed dramatically and large-scale assessments have come a long way in their use of scores on tests since the early part of the 20th century. Yet even now, the mere mention of the terms *large-scale assessment* or *standardized assessment* prompts criticisms to which assessment experts must respond (see Phelps, 2009).

The Place of Classroom Assessment

An obvious question is, What is the rightful place of CA? Discussions regarding current uses of CA typically emphasize their inherent value and the advantages they provide over large-scale assessments. For example, McMillan (2013b) notes:

> It is more than mere measurement or quantification of student performance. CA connects learning targets to effective assessment practices teachers use in their classrooms to monitor and improve student learning. When CA is integrated with and related to learning, motivation, and curriculum it both educates students and improves their learning. (p. 4)

Bruce Randel and Tedra Clark (2013) explain that CAs "play a key role in the classroom instruction and learning" (p. 161). Susan M. Brookhart (2013) explains that CAs can be a strong motivational tool when used appropriately. M. Christina Schneider, Karla L. Egan, and Marc W. Julian (2013) identify CA as one of three components of a comprehensive assessments system. Figure I.1 depicts the relationship among these three systems.

Classroom Assessments	□□□□□□□□□□ ↓↓↓↓↓↓↓↓↓↓	Standards
Interim Assessments	□□□□ ↓↓↓↓	
Year-End Assessments	□	

Figure I.1: The three systems of assessment.

As depicted in figure I.1, CAs are the first line of data about students. They provide ongoing evidence about students' current status on specific topics derived from standards. Additionally, according to figure I.1, CAs should be the most frequently used form of assessments.

Next are *interim assessments*. Schneider and colleagues (2013) describe them as follows: "Interim assessments (sometimes referred to as benchmark assessments) are standardized, periodic assessments of students throughout a school year or subject course" (p. 58).

Year-end assessments are the least frequent type of assessments employed in schools. Schneider and colleagues (2013) describe them in the following way:

> States administer year-end assessments to gauge how well schools and districts are performing with respect to the state standards. These tests are broad in scope because test content is cumulative and sampled across the state-level content standards to support inferences regarding how much a student can do in relation to all of the state standards. Simply

stated, these are summative tests. The term *year-end assessment* can be a misnomer because these assessments are sometimes administered toward the end of a school year, usually in March or April and sometimes during the first semester of the school year. (p. 59)

While CAs have a prominent place in discussions about comprehensive assessments, they have continually exhibited weaknesses that limit their use or, at least, the confidence in their interpretation. For example, Cynthia Campbell (2013) notes the "research investigating evaluation practices of classroom teachers has consistently reported concerns about the adequacy of their assessment knowledge and skill" (p. 71). Campbell (2013) lists a variety of concerns about teachers' design and use of CAs, including the following.

- Teachers have little or no preparation for designing and using classroom assessments.

- Teachers' grading practices are idiosyncratic and erratic.

- Teachers have erroneous beliefs about effective assessment.

- Teachers make little use of the variety of assessment practices available.

- Teachers don't spend adequate time preparing and vetting classroom assessments.

- Teachers' evaluative judgments are generally imprecise.

Clearly, CAs are important, and researchers widely acknowledge their potential role in the overall assessment scheme. But there are many issues that must be addressed before CAs can assume their rightful role in the education process.

Reliability and Validity at the Heart of the Matter

Almost all problems associated with CAs find their ultimate source in the concepts of reliability and validity. *Reliability* is generally described as the accuracy of a measurement. *Validity* is generally thought of as the extent to which an assessment measures what it purports to measure.

Reliability and validity are related in a variety of ways (discussed in depth in subsequent chapters). Even on the surface, though, it makes intuitive sense that validity is probably the first order of business when designing an assessment; if a test doesn't measure what it is supposed to measure, it is of little use. However, even if a test is designed with great attention to its validity, its reliability can render validity a moot point.

An assessment's validity can be limited or mediated by its reliability (Bonner, 2013; Parkes, 2013). For example, imagine you were trying to develop an instrument that measures weight. This is a pretty straightforward construct, in that weight is defined as the amount of gravitational pull on an object or the force on an object due to gravity. With this clear goal in mind, you create your own version of a scale, but unfortunately, it gives different measurements each time an object is placed on it. You put an object on it, and it indicates that the object weighs one pound. You take it off and put it on again, and it reads one and a half pounds. The third time, it reads three-quarters of a pound, and so on. Even though the measurement device was focused on weight, the score derived from the measurement process is so inaccurate (imprecise or unreliable) that it cannot be a true measure of weight. Hence, your scale cannot produce valid measures of weight even though you designed it for that specific purpose. Its reliability has limited its validity. This is probably the reason that reliability seems to receive the majority of the attention in discussions of CA. If a test is not reliable, its validity is negated.

The Need for New Paradigms

For CAs to take their rightful place in the assessment triad depicted in figure I.1, they must be both valid and reliable. This is not a new or shocking idea; reliability and validity for CAs must be thought of differently from how they are with large-scale assessments.

Large-scale assessments are so different from CAs in structure and function that the paradigms for validity and reliability developed for large-scale assessments do not apply well to CAs. There are some who argue that they are so different from large-scale assessments that they should be held to a different standard than large-scale assessments. For example, Jay Parkes (2013) notes, "There have also been those who argue that CAs . . . have such strong validity that we should tolerate low reliability" (p. 113).

While I believe this is a defensible perspective, in this book, I take the position that we should not simply ignore psychometric concepts related to validity and reliability. Rather, we should hold CAs accountable to high standards relative to both validity and reliability, but educators should reconceptualize the standards and psychometric constructs on which these standards are based in order to fit the unique environment of the classroom. I also believe that technical advances in CA have been hindered because of the unquestioned adherence to the measurement paradigms developed for large-scale assessments.

The Large-Scale Assessment Paradigm for Reliability

Even though validity is the first order of business when designing an assessment, I begin with a discussion of reliability because of the emphasis it receives in the literature on CAs. At its core, *reliability* refers to the accuracy of a measurement, where *accuracy* refers to how much or how little error exists in an individual score from an assessment. In practice, though, large-scale assessments represent reliability in terms of scores for groups of students as opposed to individual students. (For ease of discussion, I will use the terms *large-scale* and *traditional* as synonyms throughout the text.) As we shall see in chapter 4 (page 83), the conceptual formula for reliability in the large-scale assessment paradigm is based on differences in scores across multiple administrations of a test. Consider table I.1 to illustrate the traditional concept of reliability.

The column Initial Administration reports the scores of ten students for the first administration of a specific test. (For ease of discussion, the scores are listed in rank order.) The next column, Second Administration (A), and the first represent a pattern of scores that indicate relatively high reliability for the test in question.

Table I.1: Three Administrations of the Same Test

	Initial Administration	Second Administration (A)	Second Administration (B)
Student 1	97	98	82
Student 2	92	90	84
Student 3	86	80	79
Student 4	83	83	72
Student 5	81	79	66
Student 6	80	83	70
Student 7	78	78	66
Student 8	77	74	55
Student 9	70	68	88
Student 10	65	66	78

To understand this pattern, one must imagine that the second administration happened right after the initial administration, but somehow students forgot how they answered the items the first time. In fact, it's best to imagine that students forgot they took the test in the first place. Although this is impossible in real life, it is a basic theoretical underpinning of the traditional concept of reliability—the pattern of scores that would occur across students over multiple replications of the same assessment. Lee J. Cronbach and Richard J. Shavelson (2004) explain this unusual assumption in the following way:

> If, hypothetically, we could apply the instrument twice and on the second occasion have the person unchanged and without memory of his first experience, then the consistency of the two identical measurements would indicate the uncertainty due to measurement error. (p. 394)

If a test is reliable, one would expect students to get close to the same scores on the second administration of the test as they did on the first. As depicted in Second Administration (A), this is basically the case. Even though only two students received exactly the same score, all scores in the second administration were very close to their counterparts in the first.

If a test is unreliable, however, one would expect students to receive scores on the second administration that are substantially different from those they received on the first. This is depicted in the column Second Administration (B). Notice that students' scores vary greatly from their first on this hypothetical administration.

Table I.1 demonstrates the general process at a conceptual level of determining reliability from a traditional perspective. If the pattern of variation in scores among students is the same from one administration of a test to another, then the test is deemed reliable. If the pattern of variation changes from administration to administration, the test is not considered reliable. Of course, administrations of the same tests to the same students without students remembering their previous answers don't occur in real life. Consequently, measurement experts (called *psychometricians*) have developed formulas that provide reliability estimates from a single administration of a test. I discuss this in chapter 3 (page 59).

Next, we consider the equation for a single score, as well as the reliability coefficient.

The Equation for a Single Score

While the large-scale paradigm considers reliability from the perspective of a pattern of scores for groups of students across multiple test administrations, it is also based on the assumption that scores for individual students contain some amount of error. Error may be due to careless mistakes on the part of students, on the part of those administering and scoring the test, or both. Such an error is referred to as a *random measurement error*, and that is an anticipated part of any assessment (Frisbie, 1988). Random error can either increase the score a student receives (referred to as the *observed score*) or decrease the score a student receives. To represent this, the conceptual equation for an individual score within the traditional paradigm is:

Observed score = true score + error score

The true score is the score a test taker would receive if there were no random errors from the test or the test taker. In effect, the equation implies that when anyone receives a score on any type of assessment, there is no guarantee that the score the test taker receives (for example, the observed score) is the true score. The true score might be slightly or greatly higher or lower than the observed score.

The Reliability Coefficient

The reliability of an assessment from the traditional perspective is commonly expressed as an index of reliability—also referred to as the *reliability coefficient* (Kelley, 1942). Such a coefficient ranges from a 0.00 to a 1.00, with 1.00 meaning there is no random error operating in an assessment, and 0.00 indicating that the test scores completely comprise random error. While there are no published tests with a reliability of 1.00 (simply because it's impossible to construct such a test), there are also none published with a reliability even remotely close to 0.00. Indeed, David A. Frisbie (1988) notes that most published tests have reliabilities of about 0.90, but most teacher-designed tests have much lower reliabilities of about 0.50. Others have reported higher reliabilities for teacher-designed assessments (for example, Kinyua & Okunya, 2014). Leonard S. Feldt and Robert L. Brennan (1993) add a cautionary note to the practice of judging an assessment from its reliability coefficient:

> Although all such standards are arbitrary, most users believe, with considerable support from textbook authors, that instruments with coefficients lower than 0.70 are not well suited to individual student evaluations. Although one may quarrel with any standard of this sort, many knowledgeable test users adjust their level of confidence in measurement data as a hazy function of the magnitude of the reliability coefficient. (p. 106)

As discussed earlier, the reliability coefficient tells us how much a set of scores for the same students would differ from administration to administration, but it tells us very little about the scores for individual students. The only way to examine the precision of individual scores is to calculate a confidence interval around the observed scores. Confidence intervals are described in detail in technical note I.1 (page 110), but conceptually they can be illustrated rather easily. To do so, table I.2 depicts the 95 percent confidence interval around an observed score of seventy-five out of one hundred points for tests with reliabilities ranging from 0.55 to 0.85.

Table I.2: Ninety-Five Percent Confidence Intervals for Observed Score of 75

Reliability	Observed Score	Lower Limit	Upper Limit	Range
0.85	75	69	81	12
0.75	75	67	83	16
0.65	75	65	85	20
0.55	75	64	86	22

Note: The standard deviation of this test was 8.33 and the upper and lower limits have been rounded.

Table I.2 depicts a rather disappointing situation. Even when a test has a reliability of 0.85, an observed score of 75 has a 95 percent confidence interval of 69 to 81. When the reliability is as low as 0.55, then that confidence interval is between 64 and 86. From this perspective, CAs appear almost useless in that they have so much random error associated with them. Fortunately, there is another perspective on reliability to use to render CAs more precise and, therefore, more useful.

The New CA Paradigm for Reliability

As long as the reliabilities of CAs are determined using the coefficients of reliability based on formulas that examine the difference in patterns of scores between students, there is little chance of teachers being able to demonstrate the precision of their assessments for individual students. These traditional formulas typically require a great many items and a great many examinees to use in a meaningful way. Classroom teachers usually have relatively few items on their tests (which are administered to relatively few students).

This problem is solved, however, if we consider CAs in sets administered over time. The perspective of reliability calculated from sets of assessments administered over time has been in the literature for decades (see Rogosa, Brandt, & Zimowski, 1982; Willett, 1985, 1988). Specifically, a central tenet of this book is that one should examine reliability of CAs from the perspective of groups of assessments on the same topic administered over time (as opposed to a single assessment at one point in time). To illustrate, consider the following five scores, each from a separate assessment, on the same topic, and administered to a specific student over time (such as a grading period): 71, 75, 81, 79, 84.

We must analyze the pattern that these scores exemplify to determine the reliability or precision of the student's scores across the set. This requires a new foundational equation from the one used in traditional assessment. That new equation must account for the timing of an assessment. The basic equation for analyzing student learning over time is:

Observed score = time of assessment (true score) + error

The part of the equation added to the basic equation from traditional assessment is that the true score for a particular student on a particular test is at a particular time. A student's true score, then, changes from assessment to assessment. Time is now a factor in any analysis of the reliability of CAs, and there is no need to assume that students have not changed from assessment to assessment.

As we administer more CAs to a student on the same topic, we have more evidence about the student's increasing true score. Additionally, we can track the student's growth over time. Finally, using this time-based approach, the pattern of scores for an individual student can be analyzed mathematically to compile the best estimates of the student's true scores on each of the tests in the set. Consider figure I.2.

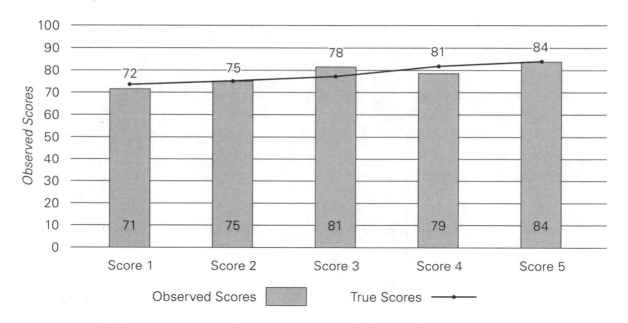

Figure I.2: Linear trend for five scores over time from an individual student.

Note that there are five bars and a line cutting across those bars. The five vertical bars represent the individual student's observed scores on five assessments administered on one topic over a given period of time (let's say a nine-week grading period).

Normally, an average of these five scores is computed to represent the student's final score for the grading period. In this case, the average of the five scores is 78. This doesn't seem to reflect the student's learning, however, because three of the observed scores were higher than this average. Alternatively, the first four scores might be thought of as formative practice only. In this case, the last score of 84 is considered the summative, and it would be the only one reported. But if we consider this single final assessment in isolation, we also must consider the error associated with it. As shown in table I.2, even if the assessment had a reliability coefficient of 0.85, we would have to add and subtract six points to be surer of the student's true score. That range of scores within the 95 percent confidence interval would be 78 to 90.

Using the new paradigm for CAs and the new time-based equation, estimates of the true score on each assessment can be made. This is what the line cutting through the five bars represents. The student's observed score on the first test was 71, but the estimated true score was 72. The second observed score was 75, as was the estimated true score, and so on.

We consider how this line and others are computed in depth in chapter 4 (page 83), but here the point is that analyzing sets of scores for the same student on the same topic over time allows us to make estimations of the student's true scores as opposed to using the observed scores only. When we report a final summative score for the student, we can do so with much more assuredness. In this case, the observed final score of 84 is the same as the predicted score, but now we have the evidence of the previous four assessments to support the precision of that summative score.

This approach also allows us to see how much a student has learned. In this case, the student's first score was 71, and his last score was 84, for a gain of thirteen points. Finally, chapter 3 (page 59) presents ways that do not rely on complex mathematical calculations to make estimates of students' true scores across a set of assessments. I address the issue of measuring student growth in chapters 3 and 4. This book also presents formulas that allow educators to program readily available tools like Excel to perform all calculations.

The Large-Scale Assessment Paradigm for Validity

The general definition for the validity of an assessment is that it measures what it is designed to measure. For large-scale assessments, this tends to create a problem from the outset since most large-scale assessments are designed to measure entire subject areas for a particular grade level. For example, a state test in English language arts (ELA) at the eighth-grade level is designed to measure all the content taught at that level. A quick analysis of the content in eighth-grade ELA demonstrates the problem.

According to Robert J. Marzano, David C. Yanoski, Jan K. Hoegh, and Julia A. Simms (2013), there are seventy-three eighth-grade topics for ELA in the CCSS. Researchers and educators refer to these as *elements*. Each of these elements contains multiple embedded topics, which means that a large-scale assessment must have multiple sections to be considered a valid measure of those topics.

Of course, sampling techniques would allow large-scale test designers to address a smaller subset of the seventy-three elements. However, validity is still a concern. To cover even a representative sample of the important content would require a test that is too long to be of practical use. As an example, assume that a test was designed to measure thirty-five (about half) of the seventy-three ELA elements for grade 8. Even if each element had only five items, the test would still contain 175 items, rendering it impractical for classroom use.

The New CA Paradigm for Validity

Relative to validity, CAs have an advantage over large-scale assessments in that they can and should be focused on a single topic (technically referred to as a single dimension). In fact, making assessments highly focused in terms of the content they address is a long-standing recommendation from the assessment community to increase validity (see Kane, 2011; Reckase, 1995). This makes intuitive sense. Since CAs will generally focus on one topic or dimension over a relatively short period, teachers can more easily ensure that they have acceptable levels of validity. Indeed, recall from the previous discussion that some measurement experts contend that CAs have such high levels of validity that we should not be concerned about their seemingly poor reliability.

The aspect of CA validity that is more difficult to address is that all tests within a set must measure precisely the same topic and contain items at the same levels of difficulty. This requirement is obvious if one examines the scores depicted in figure I.2. If these scores are to truly depict a given student's increase in his or her true score for the topic being measured, then educators must design the tests to be as identical as possible. If for example, the fourth test in figure I.2 is much more difficult than the third test, a given student's observed score on that fourth test will be lower than the score on the third test even though the student's true score has increased (the student has learned relative to the topic of the tests).

Sets of tests designed to be close to one another in the topic measured and the levels of difficulty of the items are referred to as *parallel tests*. In more technical terms, parallel tests measure the same topic and have the same types of items both in format and difficulty levels. I address how to design parallel tests in depth in chapters 2 and 3 (pages 39 and 59, respectively). Briefly, though, the more specific teachers are regarding the content students are to master and the various levels of difficulty, the easier it is for them to design parallel tests. To do this, a teacher designing a test must describe in adequate detail not only the content that demonstrates proficiency for a specific standard but also simpler content that will be directly taught and is foundational to demonstrating proficiency. Additionally, it is important to articulate what a student needs to know and do to demonstrate competence beyond the target level of proficiency. To illustrate, consider the following topic that might be the target for third-grade science.

> Students will understand how magnetic forces can affect two objects not in contact with one another.

To make this topic clear enough that teachers can design multiple assessments that are basically the same in terms of the content and its levels of difficulty, it is necessary to expand this to a level of detail depicted in table I.3, which provides three levels of content for the topic. The target level clearly describes what students must do to demonstrate proficiency. The basic level identifies important, directly taught vocabulary and basic processes. Finally, the advanced level describes a task that demonstrates students' ability to apply the target content.

Table I.3: Three Levels of Difficulty for Topic

Level of Content	Content
Advanced	Students will design a device that uses magnets to solve a problem. For example, students will be asked to identify a problem that could be solved using the attracting and repelling qualities of magnets, and create a prototype of design.
Target	Students will learn how magnetic forces can affect two objects not in contact with one another. For example, students will determine how magnets interact with other objects (including different and similar poles of other magnets), and experiment with variables that affect these interactions (such as orientation of magnets and distance between material or objects).
Basic	Students will recognize or recall specific vocabulary, such as *attraction*, *bar magnet*, *horseshoe magnet*, *magnetic field*, *magnetic*, *nonmagnetic*, *north pole*, or *south pole*. Students will perform basic processes, such as: • Explain that magnets create areas of magnetic force around them • Explain that magnets always have north and south poles • Provide example of magnetic and nonmagnetic materials • Explain how two opposite poles interact (attracting) and two opposite poles interact (repelling) • Identify variables that affect strength of magnetic force (for example, distance between objects, or size)

Source: Adapted from Simms, 2016.

The teacher now has three levels of content, all on the same topic, that provide specific directions on how to create classroom assessments on the same topic and the same levels of difficulty. I discuss how classroom teachers can do this in chapter 2 (page 39).

What to Expect in This Book

Teachers and administrators for grades K–12 will learn how to revamp the concepts of validity and reliability so they match the technical advances made in CA, instead of matching large-scale assessment's traditional paradigms for validity and reliability. This introduction lays the foundation. It introduces the new validity and reliability paradigms constructed for CAs. Chapters 1–5 describe these paradigms in detail. Chapter 1 covers the new CA paradigm for validity, noting the qualities of three major types of validity and two perspectives teachers can take regarding classroom assessments. Chapter 2 then conveys the variety of CAs that teachers can use to construct parallel assessments, which measure students' individual growth. Chapter 3 addresses the new CA paradigm for reliability and how it shifts from the traditional conception of reliability; it presents three mathematical models of reliability. Then, chapter 4 expresses how to measure groups of students' comparative growth and what purposes this serves. Finally, chapter 5 considers helpful changes to report cards and teacher evaluations based on the new paradigms for CAs. The appendix features formulas that teachers, schools, and districts can use to compute the reliability of CAs in a manner that is comparable to the level of precision offered by large-scale assessments.

chapter 1

Discussing the Classroom Assessment Paradigm for Validity

Validity is certainly the first order of business when researchers or educators design CAs. The concept of validity has evolved over the years into a multifaceted construct. As mentioned previously, the initial conception of a test's validity was that it measures what it purports to measure. As Henry E. Garrett (1937) notes, "the fidelity with which [a test] measures what it purports to measure" (p. 324) is the hallmark of its validity. By the 1950s, though, important distinctions emerged about the nature and function of validity. Samuel Messick (1993) explains that since the early 1950s, validity has been thought of as involving three major types: (1) criterion-related validity, (2) construct validity, and (3) content validity.

While the three types of validity have unique qualities, these distinctions are made more complex by virtue of the fact that one can examine validity from two perspectives. John D. Hathcoat (2013) explains that these perspectives are (1) the instrumental perspective and (2) the argument-based perspective. Validity in general—and the three different types in particular—look quite different depending on the perspective. This is a central theme of this chapter, and I make a case for the argument-based perspective as superior, particularly as it relates to CAs. The chapter also covers the following topics.

- Standards as the basis of CA validity
- Dimensionality
- Measurement topics and proficiency scales
- The rise of learning progressions
- The structure of proficiency scales
- The school's role in criterion-related validity
- The nature of parallel assessments
- The measurement process

I begin by discussing the instrumental perspective and its treatment of the three types of validity.

The Instrumental Perspective

The instrumental perspective focuses on the test itself. According to Hathcoat (2013), this has been the traditional perspective in measurement theory: a specific test is deemed valid to one degree or another. All three types of validity, then, are considered aspects of a specific test that has been or is being developed within the instrumental perspective. A test possesses certain degrees of the three types of validity.

For quite some time, measurement experts have warned that the instrumental perspective invites misinterpretations of assessments. For example, in his article "Measurement 101: Some Fundamentals Revisited," Frisbie (2005) provides concrete examples of the dangers of a literal adherence to an instrumental perspective. About validity, he notes, "Validity is not about instruments themselves, but it is about score interpretations and uses" (p. 22). In effect, Frisbie notes that it is technically inaccurate to refer to the validity of a particular test. Instead, discussion should focus on the valid use or interpretation of the scores from a particular test. To illustrate the lack of adherence to this principle, he offers examples of inaccurate statements about validity from published tests:

1. "You can help ensure that the test will be valid and equitable for all students." (From an examiner's manual for a statewide assessment program, 2005)

2. "Evidence of test validity . . . should be made publicly available." (From a major publication of a prominent testing organization, 2002)

3. "In the assessment realm, this is referred to as the validity of the test." (From an introductory assessment textbook, 2005)

4. "[Test name] has proven itself in use for more than 50 years as a . . . valid test." (From the website of a prominent test publisher, 2005)

5. "Such efforts represent the cornerstone of test validity." (From the technical manual of a prominent achievement test, 2003). (Frisbie, 2005, p. 22)

Challenges like that presented by Frisbie notwithstanding, the instrumental perspective still dominates.

Criterion-related validity, construct validity, and content validity contain certain requirements if a test is deemed valid from the instrumental perspective. To establish criterion-related validity for an assessment from the instrumental perspective, a researcher typically computes a correlation coefficient between the newly developed test and some other assessment considered to already be a valid measure of the topic. This second assessment is referred to as the *criterion measure*; hence the term *criterion-related validity*. A test is considered valid for any criterion it predicts accurately (Guilford, 1946).

The major problem with criterion-related validity is that it is difficult in some cases to identify an appropriate criterion measure. Citing the work of Roderick M. Chisholm (1973), Hathcoat (2013) exemplifies the criterion problem using the ability to determine the quality of apples:

> If we wish to identify apple quality then we need a criterion to distinguish "good" apples from "bad" apples. We may choose to sort apples into

different piles based upon their color, though any criterion is adequate for this example. The problem arises whenever we ask whether our criterion worked in that color actually separated good apples from bad apples. How can we investigate our criterion without already knowing something about which apples are good and bad? (pp. 2–3)

In effect, identifying an appropriate criterion measure renders criterion-related validity very difficult for test designers in general and for classroom teachers in particular.

Construct validity became prominent about halfway through the 1900s. According to Hathcoat (2013), a seminal article in 1955 by Lee J. Cronbach and Paul E. Meehl led to a focus on construct validity. Hathcoat (2013) notes that "Cronbach and Meehl were concerned about situations wherein a target domain and/or a relevant criterion remained ambiguous" (p. 3).

Cronbach and Meehl (1955) were saying that construct validity must be established for any type of content for which it is difficult to find a criterion measure (as cited in Hathcoat, 2013). For example, where it is rather easy to find a criterion measure for content like fifth-grade geometry, it is quite difficult to find criterion measures for content like students' abilities to apply knowledge in unique situations or students' abilities to make good decisions. Any instrument designed to measure these topics must establish construct validity evidence of what such an ability entails.

In the middle of the 20th century, around the same time Cronbach and Meehl (1955) established the need for construct validity, statistical procedures became readily available that allowed psychometricians to induce the nature of an otherwise ambiguous construct. One such statistical procedure is factor analysis, which mathematically provides evidence that specific items on a test measure the same construct. (For a technical discussion of factor analysis, see Kline, 1994.) This type of analysis is also beyond the resources of the typical classroom teacher. In fact, from the perspective of the classroom teacher, construct validity is probably more a function of the standard that he or she is trying to assess than the assessment he or she is designing. For example, assume a teacher is trying to design an assessment for the following standard: "Students will be able to work effectively in cooperative teams." Construct validity would address the extent to which this standard represents a definable set of knowledge and skill—something that could actually be taught and measured.

For criterion-related validity and construct validity, the classroom teacher has few, if any, resources to address them. However, the classroom teacher can address content validity, which basically reaffirms the early definition of validity—the test measures what it is purported to measure. For the classroom teacher, this simply involves ensuring that the CA addresses the content in the standard that is the focus of instruction and assessment.

In summary, from the instrumental perspective, the classroom teacher has limited or no control over two of the three types of validity associated with CAs he or she is designing. However, from the argument-based perspective, the teacher has some control over all three types of validity.

The Argument-Based Perspective

The argument-based perspective of validity is relatively new. Although it can be traced back to work in the 1970s and 1980s around the importance of test interpretation articulated by Messick (1975, 1993), the argument-based approach became popular because of a series of works by Michael T. Kane (1992, 2001, 2009). At its core, argument-based validity involves an interpretive argument that "lays out the network of inferences leading from the test scores to the conclusions to be drawn and any decisions to be based on these conclusions" (Kane, 2001, p. 329).

From the instrumental perspective, it is the assessment itself that possesses a specific type of validity (criterion, construct, or content). In contrast, from the argument-based perspective, validity is a function of how the data generated from the assessment are used to craft an argument regarding a particular student's knowledge or skill. This type of validity applies nicely to the classroom teacher.

From the argument-based perspective, then, criterion-related validity for a CA is determined by a teacher's ability to use data from the assessment to predict students' performance on interim assessments and end-of-course assessments. If students do well on the CAs for a particular topic, they should also do well on the more formal assessments on that topic designed outside of the classroom.

Construct validity for CAs is determined by the extent to which a teacher can use data from these assessments to identify specific knowledge and skills that should be directly taught. If a teacher can translate scores on the CAs into specific types of instruction for specific students on specific content, then the information generated from the CAs is judged to have construct validity.

From the argument-based perspective, content validity for CAs is determined by a teacher's ability to use the information generated from CAs as evidence regarding students' current knowledge and skill on a specific topic. If the teacher can use the scores on the CAs to determine what content students know and what content they don't know on a specific progression of knowledge, then the information generated from the CAs is judged to have content validity.

The distinction between the instrumental and argument-based perspectives is critical to establishing the validity of CAs. Table 1.1 summarizes these differences.

Table 1.1: CA Validity From the Instrumental and Argument-Based Perspectives

Validity Type	Instrumental Perspective	Argument-Based Perspective
Criterion-Related Validity	Scores on a specific CA are correlated highly with scores on some external assessment of the content already established as valid.	The information provided by a set of CAs can be interpretable in terms of how well students might perform on interim and end-of-year assessments.
Construct Validity	Based on statistical analysis, the items on a particular CA are highly correlated for a particular topic.	The information provided by a set of CAs can be interpretable in terms of specific knowledge or skill that can be directly taught.

Content Validity	The scores on a specific CA clearly measure specific content.	The information provided by a set of CAs can be interpreted in terms of students' status on an explicit progression of knowledge.

The argument-based perspective is perfectly suited for classroom teachers, and classroom teachers are the perfect individuals to generate Kane's (1992, 2001, 2009) network of inferences leading to conclusions and decisions from the scores generated from CAs. To do this effectively, though, teachers must utilize standards as the basis for designing tests.

Standards as the Basis of CA Validity

As the discussion in the introduction illustrates, CAs have an advantage over traditional assessments in that they typically have a narrow focus. Also, within K–12 education, the topics on which CAs should focus have been articulated in content standards. This would seem to make the various types of validity relatively easy for classroom teachers, and it does so if standards are used wisely. Unfortunately, state standards usually require a great deal of interpretation and adaptation to be used effectively in guiding the development of CAs. Their interpretations make all the difference in the world in terms of the utility of standards. As Schneider et al. (2013) note, the way educators interpret state standards plays a major role in assessment development.

Now we consider the standards movement, as well as the problem with standards.

The Standards Movement

The K–12 standards movement in the United States has a long, intriguing history. (For a detailed discussion, see Marzano & Haystead, 2008; Marzano et al., 2013). Arguably, the standards movement started in 1989 at the first education summit when the National Education Goals Panel (1991, 1993) set national goals for the year 2000. Millions of dollars were made available to develop sample national standards in all the major subject areas. States took these national-level documents and created state-level versions. Probably the most famous attempts to influence state standards at the national level came in the form of the CCSS and the Next Generation Science Standards (NGSS). States have continued to adapt national-level documents such as these to meet the needs and values of their constituents.

The Problem With Standards

While it might appear that standards help teachers design valid CAs (at least in terms of content validity), this is not necessarily the case. In fact, in many situations, state standards make validity of all types problematic to achieve. To illustrate, consider the following Common Core State Standard for eighth-grade reading: "Determine the meaning of words and phrases as they are used in a text, including figurative, connotative, and technical meanings; analyze the impact of specific word choices on meaning and tone, including analogies or allusions to other texts" (RI.8.4; NGA & CCSSO, 2010a, p. 39).

While this standard provides some direction for assessment development, it contains a great deal of content. Specifically, this standard includes the following information and skills.

- Students will understand what figurative, connotative, and technical meanings are.
- Students will be able to identify specific word choices an author made.
- Students will be able to analyze the impact of specific word choices.
- Students will understand what tone is.
- Students will understand what an analogy is.
- Students will understand what an allusion is.
- Students will be able to analyze analogies and allusions.

The volume of discrete pieces of content in this one standard creates an obvious problem of too much content. As mentioned previously, in their analysis of the CCSS, Marzano et al. (2013) identify seventy-three standard statements for eighth-grade English language arts, as articulated in the CCSS. If one makes a conservative assumption that each of those statements contains about seven component skills like those listed previously, this would mean that an eighth-grade teacher is expected to assess 365 specific pieces of content for ELA alone in a 180-day school year. According to Marzano and colleagues (2013), the same pattern can be observed in many state standards documents.

Given the fact that it is virtually impossible to teach all the content embedded in national or state standards for a given subject area, a teacher must unpack standards to identify what will be assessed within a system of CAs. Ideally, the district or school does this unpacking. Tammy Heflebower, Jan K. Hoegh, and Phil Warrick (2014) explain how a school or district can lead a systematic effort to identify between fifteen and twenty-five essential topics that should be the focus of CAs. Briefly, the process involves prioritizing standards and the elements within those standards that are absolutely essential to assess. When identifying and articulating essential topics in standards, schools and districts must be cognizant of their dimensionality.

Dimensionality

In general, there should be one topic addressed in a CA. Parkes (2013) explains that this is a foundational concept in measurement theory: "any single score from a measurement is to represent a single quality" (p. 107). This is technically referred to as making a CA *unidimensional* (technically stated, a unidimensional test "measures only one dimension or only one latent trait" [AERA et al., 2014, p. 224]). The notion that unidimensionality is foundational to test theory can be traced back to the middle of the 1900s. For example, in a foundational article on measurement theory in 1959, Frederic M. Lord notes that a test is a "collection of tasks; the examinee's performance on these tasks is taken as an index of [a student's] standing along some psychological dimension" (p. 473). Over forty years later, David Thissen and Howard Wainer (2001) explain:

> Before the responses to any set of items are combined into a single score
> that is taken to be, in some sense, representative of the responses to all of

the items, we must ascertain the extent to which the items "measure the same thing." (p. 10)

Without unidimensionality, a score on a test is difficult to interpret. For example, assume that two students receive a score of 70 on the same test, but that test measures two dimensions. This is depicted in figure 1.1.

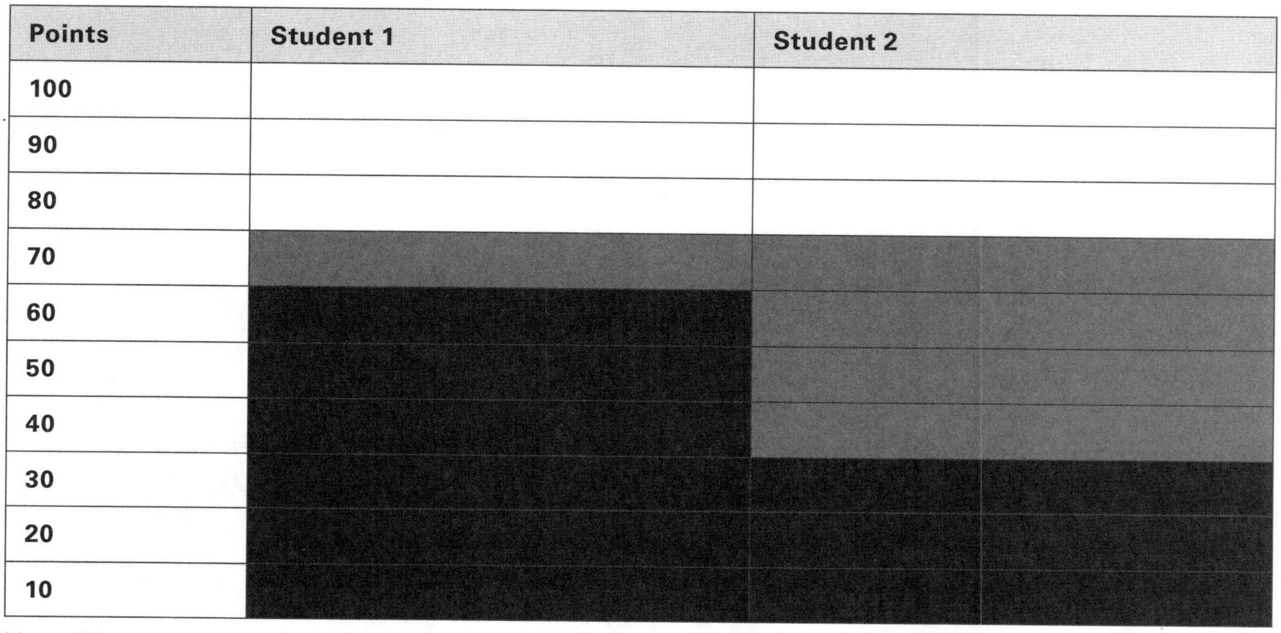

Points	Student 1	Student 2
100		
90		
80		
70		
60		
50		
40		
30		
20		
10		

Note: Black = patterns; gray = data analysis. Total possible points for black (patterns) = sixty; total possible points for gray (data analysis) = forty.

Figure 1.1: Two students' scores on a two-dimensional test.

In figure 1.1, student 1 and student 2 both receive a total score of 70 on the test, but the test was designed in such a way that sixty points were allocated to the topic (dimension) of patterns and forty points to the topic of data analysis. Student 1 received sixty out of sixty points for the topic of patterns but only ten out of forty points for the topic of data analysis. Student 2 received thirty out of sixty points for the topic of patterns and forty out of forty points for the topic of data analysis. Although both students received the same overall score, they exhibited very different profiles relative to the two dimensions embedded in the test.

As this example illustrates, the overall score on a test that measures more than one dimension is uninterpretable in terms of students' knowledge and skill regarding specific content. This is a construct validity issue. Unfortunately, even with professionally designed assessments, the requirement that all the items measure a common trait is often violated (Hattie, 1984, 1985; Hattie, Krakowski, Rogers, & Swaminathan, 1996). This does not justify teachers ignoring the need for a single dimension for CAs. Indeed, classroom teachers should always be cognizant that their tests measure the same single dimension.

One important qualifier to the rule that an assessment should focus on a single dimension is the fact that sometimes seemingly different topics covary. I discussed this topic in some depth in *Classroom Assessment and Grading That Work* (Marzano, 2006). Building on this discussion, Simms (2016) explains that "covariance means that two or more elements of knowledge or skill are so closely related that if student performance on one increases, student performance is likely to also increase for the other" (pp. 20–21). To illustrate, Simms (2016) cites the following topics from eight standards in the CCSS as examples of covarying elements:

- **Compare arguments to alternate or opposing arguments** (for example, identify similarities and differences between the claims and evidence provided by two articles featured in *The New York Times'* [2014] Room for Debate feature "Taking Sports Out of School").

- **Evaluate the relevance, sufficiency, credibility, and accuracy of evidence for a specific claim** (for example, read Terra Snider's [2014] cnn.com article "Let Kids Sleep Later" and explain why the evidence for her claim that school should start later is or is not sufficient and credible).

- **Identify errors in reasoning (i.e., logical errors, fallacies) in an argument** (for example, watch a campaign attack ad and identify how the advertisement employs unsound logic to discredit another candidate). (p. 20)

Simms (2016) notes that these three elements can be legitimately organized under the single measurement topic of Analyzing Claims, Evidence, and Reasoning because it is most probably the case that they are highly related. As skill in one element goes up, so too does skill in the other two elements, particularly if these three topics are taught together. These topics, then, are said to covary.

One indication that elements covary is that they can be integrated in the same task. Simms (2016) offers the following task as evidence that the three elements preceding covary:

> Evaluate the argument in a text by deciding if the reasoning is sound, if the claims have sufficient evidence, and if the author appropriately responds to conflicting arguments (for example, examine the argument in Charles Wilson and Eric Schlosser's [2006] book *Chew on This: Everything You Don't Want to Know About Fast Food* and determine how well the authors address opposing arguments which claim that fast food restaurants provide affordable and convenient meals). (p. 20)

Identifying essential elements from the standards, then, is not simply a matter of unpacking standards and considering each topic as a unique dimension. Rather, topics that covary do, in fact, represent a single dimension and can be included in a single assessment.

Measurement Topics and Proficiency Scales

Over the years, I have used the convention of referring to the essential topics gleaned from standards as *measurement topics* (Marzano, 2006, 2010) since they form the basis for designing CAs. In general, there should be no more than twenty-five measurement topics for a given subject at a given grade level, although I have observed schools that have more and still function quite well. To aid schools and districts in this endeavor, Simms (2016) identifies 502 measurement topics in ELA, mathematics, and science. For example, the following are the measurement topics for third-grade mathematics.

- Estimation
- Multiplication
- Division
- Word Problems
- Fractions
- Equivalent Fractions
- Fractional Measurements
- Patterns
- Time
- Mass and Liquid Volume
- Area
- Perimeter
- Two-Dimensional Figures
- Representing Categorical Data

As noted previously, these measurement topics might contain more than one element if they are deemed to covary. Each measurement topic should have a corresponding proficiency scale.

I believe that proficiency scales are absolutely necessary to the effective design of CAs. Before going into the specifics of proficiency scales, it is useful to examine their relationship with learning progressions. One might think of a proficiency scale as a specialized type of learning progression.

The Rise of Learning Progressions

One of the more powerful movements in CA has been the rise of learning progressions. While this term is used widely, it is also used in a variety of ways. Arguably, learning progressions became popular with the publication of the book *Taking Science to School* by the National Research Council (NRC) in 2007.

Heidi L. Andrade (2013) explains that learning progressions were initially conceived as models "of successively more sophisticated ways of thinking about a topic typically demonstrated by children as they learn, from naïve to expert" (p. 18). To illustrate this perspective, consider the example by Joan L. Herman and Kilchan Choi (2008):

- Student knows that floating depends on having less density than the medium.
- Student knows that floating depends on having a small density.
- Student knows that floating depends on having a small mass and a large volume.
- Student knows that floating depends on having a small mass, or student knows that floating depends on having a large volume.
- Student thinks that floating depends on having a small size, heft, or amount, or that it depends on being made out of a particular material.
- Student thinks that floating depends on being flat, hollow, filled with air, or having holes. (p. 7)

This learning progression is for the specific concept of buoyancy. A much broader perspective on learning progressions has been articulated by Margaret Heritage (2013). She notes that learning progressions should cut across several grade levels and provide guidance for a spiraling curriculum. She cites others who take this same general perspective.

- "Learning progressions are tied to big ideas, the central concepts and principles of a discipline" (Duschl, 2006, p. 116).
- "Learning progressions . . . describe successively more sophisticated ways of reasoning in a content domain that follow one another as students learn" (Smith, Wiser, Anderson, & Krajcik, 2006, p. 2).
- Vertical maps that provide "a description of skills, understanding and knowledge in the sequence in which they typically develop: a picture of what it means to 'improve' in an area of learning" (Masters & Forster, 1996, p. 1).

The Common Core State Standards (NGA & CCSSO, 2010a, 2010b) and the Next Generation Science Standards (NGSS Lead States, 2013) used this broad perspective of learning as the basis for organizing the progressions to describe the development of content from one grade level to the next.

For the purposes of CAs, however, I recommend progressions of knowledge for topics *within* grade levels, as opposed to *across* grade levels. To illustrate, Andrade (2013) offers the following example in figure 1.2 (which she adapted from Briggs, Alonzo, Schwab, & Wilson, 2006). Classroom teachers could use this learning progression effectively to design CAs.

This learning progression depicts the level of detail required to guide the development of CAs. Note that specific content is identified for each level of performance. A classroom teacher could easily construct assessment items for each of these levels. Heritage (2013) notes that learning progressions, such as that in figure 1.2, should follow the Goldilocks rule by articulating not too much or too little content.

4	Student is able to coordinate apparent and actual motion of objects in the sky. The student knows the following: • The Earth is both orbiting the sun and rotating on its axis. • The Earth fully orbits the sun once per year. • The Earth rotates on its axis once per day, causing the daylight cycle and the appearance that the sun moves across the sky. • The moon orbits the Earth once every twenty-eight days, producing the phases of the moon. Common Error: Seasons are caused by the changing distance between the Earth and the sun. Common Error: The phases of the moon are caused by a shadow of planets, the sun, or the Earth falling on the moon.
3	The student knows the following: • The Earth orbits the sun. • The moon orbits the Earth. • The Earth rotates on its axis. However, student has not put this knowledge together with an understanding of apparent motion to form explanations and may not recognize that the Earth is both rotating and orbiting simultaneously. Common Error: It gets dark at night because the Earth goes around the sun once a day.
2	The student recognizes the following: • The sun appears to move across the sky every day. • The observable shape of the moon changes every twenty-eight days. Common Error: All the motion in the sky is due to the Earth spinning on its axis. Common Error: The sun travels around the Earth. Common Error: It gets dark at night because the sun goes around the Earth once a day. Common Error: The Earth is the center of the universe.
1	The student: • Does not recognize the systematic nature of the appearances of objects in the sky. • May not recognize that the Earth is spherical. Common Error: It gets dark at night because something (for example, clouds, the atmosphere, or "darkness") covers the sun. Common Error: The phases of the moon are caused by clouds covering the moon. Common Error: The sun goes below the Earth at night.

Source: Andrade, 2013, p. 19; adapted from Briggs et al. 2006.

Figure 1.2: Learning progression.

Robert J. Marzano, Jennifer S. Norford, Michelle Finn, and Douglas Finn III (2017) address another type of scale that is becoming popular. They refer to these progressions as *scoring rubrics*. They note:

> With such an approach, students often receive very general feedback (such as *superior* on grammar and mechanics and *poor* on persuasiveness),

or they are rated according to a frequency or consistency metric (such as *occasionally* on "applying properties of operations as strategies to add and subtract rational numbers" and *rarely* on "applying properties of operations as strategies to multiply and divide rational numbers"). (p. 35)

They explain that, although they provide some specificity for scoring purposes, scoring rubrics do not delineate what a student knows regarding the target content. Another potential problem with scoring rubrics is depicted in figure 1.3.

Performance Indicator	"Develop and use a model to describe the function of a cell as a whole and ways parts of cells contribute to the function" (NGSS Lead States, 2013, MS-LS1–2).		
Emerging	**Progressing**	**Competent**	**Exemplary**
The student can state the function of each organelle in a cell.	Using an illustration of a cell, the student can identify each cell structure and describe its functions.	The student can develop and use a model to describe the function of a cell as a whole and ways parts of cells contribute to the function.	The student can create real-world analogies for the function of a cell as a whole and ways parts of cells contribute to the function.

Figure 1.3: Scoring rubric for a performance indicator.

This scoring rubric provides some information about the content students should know (for example, the function of a cell and the ways individual structures of a cell contribute to its function), but the levels of the scale narrow the assessment options available to teachers, because they are stated as activities. For example, to demonstrate the emerging level of performance, a student must "state the function of each organelle in a cell," whereas to demonstrate the progressing level, the student must use an illustration to identify the cell structures and then describe their functions. This wording locks students into specific ways they can demonstrate competence and locks teachers into specific ways they can assess it.

The Structure of Proficiency Scales

Proficiency scales have a format that has been in development since 1996 (Marzano, 2000, 2006, 2010; Marzano & Kendall, 1996). As mentioned previously, they are a type of learning progression. While they are certainly like some of the forms of learning progressions and rubrics previously described, these are designed specifically for the type of CAs described in this book. Learning progressions and rubrics are not. A teacher should be able to transform a well-designed proficiency scale into multiple assessments on a specific topic. Unlike the previous examples of learning progressions, they do not lock teachers into specific types of assessments. Indeed, as I demonstrate in chapter 2 (page 39), teachers can use a wide variety of assessment formats that are based on proficiency scales. A proficiency scale is depicted in figure 1.4.

4.0	The student will: • Use mental computation and estimation strategies to assess the reasonableness of an answer at different stages of solving a problem (for example, when given that a boy has 374 more baseball cards than a friend who has 221 baseball cards, and when given that he then buys another 186 cards, use rounding to estimate that the boy started with close to 600 baseball cards and ended up with close to 800).
3.5	In addition to score 3.0 performance, partial success at score 4.0 content
3.0	The student will: • Round a given number to the nearest 10 or 100 (for example, round the numbers 23, 50, 95, 447, 283, 509, and 962 to the nearest 10 and the nearest 100).
2.5	No major errors or omissions regarding score 2.0 content, and partial success at score 3.0 content
2.0	The student will recognize or recall specific vocabulary (for example, *digit, estimate, hundreds, number line, ones, place, place value, round, round down, round up, tens, thousands*) and perform basic processes, such as: • Identifying multiples of 10 and 100 • Identifying relationships between place values; for example, explain that ten 1s are equal to one 10 and that ten 10s are equal to one 100 • Explaining that rounding a number to a given place estimates or approximates the value of the number to the nearest multiple of that place; for example, rounding a number to the nearest 10 approximates the value of that number to the nearest multiple of 10 • Explaining that rounding a number to a given place will leave a value of 0 in each place that is smaller than (to the right of) the targeted place; for example, rounding a number to the nearest 100 will leave a value of 0 in the tens and ones places • Using a number line to find the nearest multiple of a specified place for a given number; for example, when given the number 146 represented on a number line, identify 100 as the closest multiple of 100 • Explaining that a number will be rounded up to a given place if the digit in the place immediately to the right is greater than or equal to 5, and will be rounded down if the digit is less than or equal to 4 • Identifying situations in which rounding might be useful; for example, explain that rounding two addends and quickly calculating their sum can be useful for assessing whether or not the calculated sum of the unrounded addends is accurate
1.5	Partial success at score 2.0 content, and major errors or omissions regarding score 3.0 content
1.0	With help, partial success at score 2.0 content and score 3.0 content
0.5	With help, partial success at score 2.0 content but not at score 3.0 content
0.0	Even with help, no success

Figure 1.4: Proficiency scale for measurement topic of estimation at third-grade level.

The proficiency scale in figure 1.4 is for the measurement topic of estimation for third-grade mathematics. The fulcrum of a proficiency scale is score 3.0 content. It is the desired state of knowledge or skill. In this case, that content involves rounding to the nearest 10 or 100. The score 3.0 level also provides specific examples of the content that would demonstrate proficiency. Score 2.0 contains important vocabulary that will be taught directly. It also identifies basic skills that will be addressed specifically, like identifying multiples of 10 and 100. The score 4.0 content involves an example of a specific task that could be used to demonstrate competency beyond proficiency.

These three levels of proficiency are designed to make CA construction relatively easy, and the scale can help teachers design multiple types of assessments. A proficiency scale, then, does not limit the types of assessments that can be designed from it. As Carol Bereiter (1963) notes, it is senseless to consider a "test a valid instrument of an attribute that is not clearly conceptualized independently of any instrument supposed to measure it" (p. 13). Proficiency scales do just that.

In addition to the three levels of content for a given measurement topic, proficiency scales also contain score values of 1.0 and 0.0, but these do not involve new content. Rather, a score value of 1.0 indicates that a student has partial success with score 2.0 and 3.0 content with help. The score value of 0.0 indicates that even with help, a student does not demonstrate even partial success with any of the content. Student performances that indicate half-point scores are also identified. The half point indicates partial movement to the next level of the scale. For example, a score of 2.5 indicates that a student has partial competence with the score 3.0 content. For a more detailed discussion of half-point and full-point scores, see Marzano (2006).

In effect, the three levels of explicit content (that is, score values 2.0, 3.0, and 4.0) can be translated into nine different score values based on evidence provided by a CA. This is the essence of the argument-based approach to validity.

When designing proficiency scales, it is important to remember the concepts of unidimensionality and covariance. As discussed previously, a proficiency scale can include multiple elements if it is determined that they covary. For example, consider the proficiency scale in figure 1.5 that might be created for the covarying elements described previously.

4.0	The student will:
	▪ Evaluate the argument in a text by deciding if the reasoning is sound, if the claims have sufficient evidence, and if the author appropriately responds to conflicting arguments. For example, examine the argument in Charles Wilson and Eric Schlosser's 2006 book *Chew on This: Everything You Don't Want to Know About Fast Food* and determine how well the authors address opposing arguments claiming that fast-food restaurants provide affordable and convenient meals.
3.5	In addition to score 3.0 performance, partial success at score 4.0 content
3.0	The student will:
	▪ **Compare arguments to alternate or opposing arguments.** For example, identify similarities and differences between the claims and evidence provided by two articles featured in *The New York Times'* (2014) Room for Debate feature "Taking Sports Out of School."
	▪ **Evaluate the relevance, sufficiency, credibility, and accuracy of evidence for a specific claim.** For example, read Terra Snider's (2014) cnn.com article "Let Kids Sleep Later" and explain why the evidence for her claim that school should start later is or is not sufficient and credible.

	• **Identify errors in reasoning.** Logical errors and fallacies in an argument are examples. For example, watch a campaign attack ad and identify how the advertisement employs unsound logic to discredit another candidate.
2.5	No major errors or omissions regarding score 2.0 content, and partial success at score 3.0 content

2.0	The student will:
	
	 • **Recognize or recall specific vocabulary.** Vocabulary examples include *argument*, *backing*, *claim*, *evidence*, *grounds*, *paragraph*, *qualifier*, *reasoning*, and *summarize*. Basic processes include the following.
	     ◆ Describing the parts of an argument (such as claim, grounds, backing, qualifier)
	     ◆ Explaining the role of grounds, backing, and qualifiers in a claim
	     ◆ Summarizing what each paragraph of an argument seems to be saying
	     ◆ Annotating a text's central claims and the grounds for the claims
	     ◆ Annotating the evidence, or backing, given in a text
	     ◆ Annotating qualifiers in a claim
	     ◆ Using a graphic organizer to compare the claims and evidence for two arguments
	
	 • The student will recognize or recall specific vocabulary (for example, *accurate*, *cite*, *claim*, *credible*, *evidence*, *irrelevant*, *relevant*, *source*, *sufficient*) and perform basic processes, such as:
	     ◆ Listing different kinds of evidence that texts can use (such as statistics, quotes, historical facts)
	     ◆ Describing what makes evidence relevant, sufficient, credible, and accurate
	     ◆ Outlining the evidence for a claim in a text
	     ◆ Annotating evidence in an argument that cites a source
	     ◆ Rating the strength of a piece of evidence
	
	 The student will:
	
	 • **Recognize or recall specific vocabulary.** Vocabulary examples include *argument*, *conclusion*, *fallacy*, *logic*, *premise*, *reasoning*, *premise*, *sound*, *unsound*. Basic processes include the following.
	     ◆ Describing common fallacies (such as using an overly emotional argument, false appeals to authority, and attacking the opponent instead of the argument)
	     ◆ Describing the difference between sound and unsound logic
	     ◆ Annotating words that indicate a premise (such as *since*, *because*, and *as an example*)
	     ◆ Annotating words that indicate a conclusion (such as *therefore*, *consequently*, and *thus*)
	     ◆ Outlining the logic of an argument (for example, show which premises lead to which conclusions)

1.5	Partial success at score 2.0 content, and major errors or omissions regarding score 3.0 content
1.0	With help, partial success at score 2.0 content and score 3.0 content
0.5	With help, partial success at score 2.0 content but not at score 3.0 content
0.0	Even with help, no success

Source: Simms, 2016, p. 20. Used with permission.

Figure 1.5: Proficiency scale with covarying elements.

Figure 1.5 has three elements at the score 3.0 level. In keeping, it also has three levels of basic content at the score 2.0 level. In contrast, the score 4.0 has a specific task that integrates the score 2.0 and 3.0 content. As described previously, one of the indications that elements covary is that they can be combined into a single task at the 4.0 level.

When designing CAs using this proficiency scale, a teacher would sample content across the elements—that is, CAs would not have to include content from each of the three elements at the score 2.0 level and the score 3.0 level. Because the topics were deemed to covary, content from one topic could be considered to represent content related to the other two topics. *I cannot emphasize this point enough.* When a proficiency scale includes two or more elements at the score 3.0 level, it means that those who created the scale believe that if students increase their competence in one element, their competence in the other element or elements will also increase. Thus, when assessments are designed from the scale, teachers do not have to include items for each element. Also, a single score on the scale is assigned for an assessment as opposed to a score for each element. If those who created the scale believe that a separate score should be assigned to each element, then each element should be recast as a separate proficiency scale.

The development of proficiency scales adds greatly to the development of CAs and allows teachers to use the data from their assessments in a valid manner using an argument-based approach. This is necessarily so because a proficiency scale provides a detailed description of the content that is the focus of a given assessment.

The School's Role in Criterion-Related Validity

As mentioned at the beginning of this chapter, it is difficult for classroom teachers to document the criterion-related validity of CAs. The best they can do is use performance on sets of CAs to predict how well students will perform on interim and end-of-year assessments. However, more formally establishing criterion-related validity for CAs is a relatively easy task for the school or district. Specifically, the school or district simply keeps track of the relationship between students' scores on the proficiency scales and students' scores on some external interim assessments, end-of-course assessments, or state tests. To illustrate, consider table 1.2.

Table 1.2: Validity Study in an Elementary School

Measurement Topics Mastered	Number of Students	Percent Proficient or Above
0	12	0
1	2	0
2	6	0
3	13	0
4	8	0
5	13	23

6	29	21
7	12	42
8	29	52
9	29	76
10	29	48
11	40	86
12	44	84
13	227	96

Source: Adapted from Haystead, 2016.

The data in table 1.2 represent the relationship between scores on proficiency scales and the results of a state assessment for third-grade mathematics. The first column reports the number of measurement topics on which students received a summative score of 3.0 or higher; the second column represents the number of students who received such scores.

According to the first row of table 1.2, twelve students did not receive a score of 3.0 or higher on any of the thirteen mathematics measurement topics at the third-grade level. However, the thirteenth row indicates that 227 students received such scores on all thirteen topics. The third column reports the percentage of students who received scores of proficient or higher on the state test. Of those twelve students who did not score 3.0 or higher on any of the measurement topics, none were proficient on the state test. The same can be said for those students who scored 3.0 or higher on only one, two, three, or four of the measurement topics—none demonstrated proficiency on the state test. Of the thirteen students who scored 3.0 or higher on five measurement topics, 23 percent demonstrated proficiency on the state test. At the bottom of the table, of the 227 students who scored 3.0 or higher on all thirteen measurement topics, 96 percent scored proficient or higher on the state test.

If the school or district keeps data like those in table 1.2, it will continually be able to monitor the criterion-related validity of its system of CAs.

The Nature of Parallel Assessments

Parallel assessments are an absolute necessity to the new paradigms for CAs simply because they are foundational to establishing the validity and reliability of CAs. They also allow teachers to examine student learning over time. The technical definition of a parallel assessment is: "Parallel forms: in classical test theory, strictly parallel test forms that are assumed to measure the same construct and to have the same means and the same standard deviations" (AERA et al., 2014, p. 221). In this section, I consider the general structure of parallel assessments, and in chapter 2 I address various formats for parallel assessments. Briefly, though, parallel assessments measure the same topic and have items that are at the same levels of difficulty. Theoretically, a student who takes two parallel assessments one right after the other should receive the same score on both. In the technical literature, though, assessment experts tend to focus on the psychometric properties of parallel assessments as opposed to the equivalence of the content. To illustrate, Harold Gulliksen (1950) notes that parallel tests must have "equal means, equal variances, and equal intercorrelations" (p. 173). Paul Horst (1966) notes that parallel tests should be equated on six dimensions: (1) number of items, (2) item difficulties, (3) the means of item difficulties, (4) the dispersion of item difficulties, (5) item variances, and (6) item covariances. David Magnusson (1967) and Frederic M. Lord and Melvin R. Novick (1968) offer similar definitions. The emphasis on defining parallel tests in terms of psychometric properties as opposed to content properties has continued since the publication of these early works (for example, Brennan, 2006; Lindquist, 1951; Linn, 1993; Thorndike, 1971).

An individual teacher probably does not have the resources to design parallel tests in such a technical manner, but he or she can design tests that have sets of items at approximately the same levels of difficulty. Proficiency scales are the best tools available to teachers to this end. To illustrate, reconsider the proficiency scale in figure 1.4 (page 29) on the topic of estimation in the third grade. The score 2.0 content includes explicit vocabulary and basic processes. To design two parallel tests, a teacher would ensure sections on both tests that assessed similar—but not identical—vocabulary terms. One test may include the following vocabulary terms: *digit*, *estimate*, *number line*, and *place value*. The other test might include the following terms: *digit*, *place value*, *round down*, and *round up*. In terms of basic processes at the 2.0 level, one test might include items that involve three of the bulleted items in the proficiency scale. The second assessment might include one identical bulleted item at the score 2.0 level and two unique items. Score 3.0 follows the same pattern. At the score 4.0 level, teachers would construct similar but not identical application tasks using the example in the proficiency scale as the model. In short, when teachers have gleaned measurement topics from standards and unidimensional proficiency scales they developed for each topic, they have an explicit blueprint with which they can design parallel assessments. These assessments produce data that allow teachers to make inferences that ensure the criterion-related validity, construct validity, and content validity of their conclusions. In chapter 2 (page 39), I consider just how to design and score such tests.

The final topic that must be considered relative to the concept of argument-based validity is the measurement process.

The Measurement Process

It is in the context of the measurement process that Kane's (1992, 2001, 2009) concept of argument-based validity can be realized to its full potential. Recall that Kane (1992, 2001, 2009) says teachers should think of the information from assessments as evidence with which to build an argument for some specific interpretation of a student's competence. This is the essence of measurement.

Not many books on measurement in education and psychology actually define the term *measurement* explicitly. Those works that do formally define measurement do so in a rather abstract way. For example, S. S. Stevens (1946) defines measurement as "the assignment of numerals to things so as to represent facts and conventions about them" (p. 680). Lord and Novick (1968) define measurement as a "procedure for the assignment of numbers (scores, measurements) to specified properties of experimental units in such a way as to characterize and preserve specified relationships in the behavioral domain" (p. 17). Parkes (2013) describes measurement as an "inferential process—taking a sample of knowledge from an individual and using it to make a conclusion about his knowledge in its entirety" (p. 109).

As these definitions illustrate, most academic texts consider measurement a process. I have articulated the measurement process in a series of works (Marzano, 2006, 2010; Marzano et al., 2017). Now, I'll expand on those previous treatments.

To understand the measurement process as defined in this resource, I summarize the meaning of some terms, as table 1.3 shows.

Table 1.3: Definitions of Measurement-Related Terms

Term	Definition
Assessment	**Technical:** "Any systematic method of obtaining information used to draw inferences about characteristics of people, objects, or programs; a systematic process to measure or evaluate the characteristics or performance of individuals, programs, or other entities for purposes of drawing inferences; sometimes used synonymously with test" (AERA et al., 2014, p. 216) **Nontechnical:** Any system a teacher uses to collect information about a student's status on a progression of knowledge and skill for a measurement topic articulated in a proficiency scale
Test	**Technical:** "A collection of tasks; the examinee's performance on these tasks is taken as an index of his [a student's] standing along some psychological dimension" (Lord, 1959, p. 473) **Nontechnical:** A specific type of assessment, usually written, that involves selected-response items and short constructed-response items
Score	**Technical:** "Any specific number resulting from the assessment of an individual, such as a raw score, a scale score, an estimate of a latent variable, a production count, an absence record, a course grade, or a rating" (AERA et al., 2014, p. 223) **Nontechnical:** A number assigned to an assessment that indicates how well a student has performed on that assessment, or a number that assigns a student to a specific level on a proficiency scale
Scale	**Technical:** "The system of numbers and their units by which a value is reported on some dimension of measurement. In testing, the set of items or subsets used to measure a specific characteristic (for example, a test of verbal ability or a scale of extroversion-introversion" (AERA et al., 2014, p. 223) **Nontechnical:** A description of levels of knowledge and skill for a specific dimension within a specific content area at a specific grade level
Measurement	**Technical:** "The assignment of numerals to objects or events according to rules" (Stevens, 1946, p. 677) **Nontechnical:** The process of using an evidence-based argument to translate scores from assessments for individual students into scores on a proficiency scale

Table 1.3 provides both technical and nontechnical definitions of terms important to the measurement process. The technical definitions come from authoritative academic sources in the professional measurement literature. The nontechnical definitions are adaptations of the technical definitions to the concepts and principles articulated in this book. In the current discussion, I will use the nontechnical definitions in table 1.3.

In nontechnical terms, an *assessment* is any systematic way a teacher collects evidence regarding a student's level of knowledge or skill on a particular measurement topic. Teachers can use each type of assessment described in chapter 2 (page 39) as evidence. A *test* is a specific type of assessment that involves items or tasks. As described in chapter 2, there are assessments other than tests that a teacher might use.

A *scale* is a system of units that describes progress along some continuum. In the system described in this book, each measurement topic is accompanied by a specifically designed proficiency scale. Assessments provide evidence with which teachers place students on a scale. Measurement, then, is the process of translating the evidence provided by assessments into a number that is understandable on the proficiency scale that is being used. This, of course, is foundational to argument-based validity—an educator using the evidence an assessment provided to make inferences about student learning.

The term *score* is the most ambiguous of the set described in table 1.3. It can describe a student's status on a particular assessment, and it can also describe a student's current status on a proficiency scale. Thus, a student receives a score on an assessment that translates into a score on a proficiency scale.

To illustrate how these concepts interact in the measurement process, assume that at the beginning of a unit, a teacher gives a pencil-and-paper test on the score 2.0 content on a particular proficiency scale. The teacher assigns test scores to students using the traditional one hundred–point or percentage scale. The teacher has established a score of 80 percent as the cut score indicating that a student should receive a score of 2.0 on the proficiency scale. (A *cut score* is the point that differentiates between those who meet a specific criterion and those who do not.) Any student who receives a score of 80 percent or above on the test earns a score of 2.0 on the proficiency scale. The score of 80 on the test translates to a score of 2.0 on the proficiency scale.

A few days later, the teacher has a discussion with a specific student and asks questions about score 2.0 and 3.0 content on the proficiency scale. The discussion qualifies as an assessment because the teacher uses it to gather information about this particular student's status on a proficiency scale for a particular measurement topic. Based on this discussion, the teacher assigns a score of 2.5, which indicates that the student understands the score 2.0 content and understands some (but not all) of the score 3.0 content. The score assigned for the discussion is recorded without the need for an interim score like that from the test.

This same pattern continues throughout the unit. Some assessments involve scores specific to a particular assessment. Teachers must translate these into scores on the proficiency scale. Other assessments are immediately scored using the metric of the proficiency scale. In the case of the discussion, the teacher did not have to make a translation because he could use the evidence from the discussion to directly assign a proficiency scale score.

The concepts in figure 1.6 and the way they interact provide a new perspective on testing and assessing students.

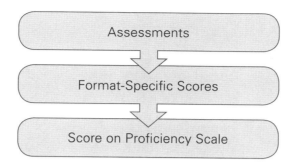

Figure 1.6: The measurement process.

Figure 1.6 demonstrates that within the measurement process, assessments produce scores that are sometimes specific to the assessment format. I refer to these scores as format-specific scores. For example, an assessment might be a quiz that yields scores from 1 to 20. An assessment might be a student presentation scored on a rubric that includes score values of excellent, proficient, progressing, and needs work. An assessment might be a rather long pencil-and-paper test that yields a score from 0 to 100. To be meaningful in terms of student learning, teachers must translate all these format-specific scores into a score on a proficiency scale.

To use Kane's (1992, 2001, 2009) terminology, the measurement process involves using data from assessments, some of which involve format-specific scores, to build a logical case as to the most appropriate score on a proficiency scale for a particular student at a particular time. Kane is one of the few assessment experts to talk about scores on assessments as data that are used to build a logical case for a more appropriate score on a scale. In general, many experts simply ignore this entire discussion which leaves the casual reader with the impression that teachers should consider a score on a single assessment in isolation and at face value.

Summary

This chapter articulates the new CA paradigm for validity, which is grounded in the argument-based perspective. This perspective treats information from assessments as evidence teachers use to construct a logical argument as to a student's score on a particular proficiency scale at a particular point in time. There are three types of validity a teacher can consider. The extent to which teachers can use students' scores on sets of CAs to predict their performance on interim and end-of-year tests constitutes criterion-related validity. The extent to which teachers can use students' scores on sets of CAs to identify concrete content that should be taught constitutes construct validity. The extent to which teachers can use students' scores on sets of CAs to place students along a continuum of knowledge constitutes content validity. To establish these types of validity, teachers should construct two things: (1) proficiency scales for each measurement topic and (2) parallel assessments designed from the proficiency scales. The chapter concludes with a description of the measurement processes that operationalizes the argument-based perspective for CAs.

Ultimately, the measurement process begins by designing and scoring parallel assessments. Chapter 2 immerses us in this process.

Designing and Scoring Parallel Assessments

For the classroom teacher, following the new validity paradigm for CAs is a continual process that sometimes involves all students in class and sometimes involves individual students. There is a variety of CAs that a teacher might use in the measurement process. Designing and scoring parallel assessments includes ten important aspects.

1. Traditional tests

2. Essays

3. Performance tasks, demonstrations, and presentations

4. Portfolios

5. Probing discussions

6. Student self-assessments

7. Assessments that cover one level of a proficiency scale

8. Complete measurement process

9. Assessment planning

10. Differentiated assessments

Traditional Tests

The term *test* is probably the most common when referring to CAs. Unfortunately, people use it in vastly different ways. Here, I restrict the meaning to assessments that are written and involve selected-response items, short constructed-response items, or both. The process of designing a traditional test, then, involves generating selected-response items and short constructed-response items that correspond to the various levels of content in a proficiency scale.

With regard to traditional tests, we must consider designing selected-response items, designing short constructed-response items, and scoring assessments that use selected-response and short constructed-response items.

Designing Selected-Response Items

Probably the most common format for an assessment that addresses all content levels of a proficiency scale is a combination of selected-response and short constructed-response items.

Selected-response items are those that require students to make a selection between alternatives. While this seems like a simple distinction, there are differences of opinion regarding whether fill-in-the-blank and completion items are selected response or constructed response (see Hogan, 2013; Rodriguez & Haladyna, 2013). For purposes of the current discussion, I classify fill-in-the-blank and completion items as selected response simply because they typically address the type and level of content associated with more obvious types of selected-response items like multiple choice. Table 2.1 lists various types of selected-response items.

Table 2.1: Selected-Response Items

Type	Example
Multiple Choice: Multiple-choice items are probably the most common type of selected-response item. These items require students to select the best answer from a set of options.	The best definition of *immigration* is: a) Driving from one country to another on vacation b) Moving from one neighborhood to another c) Traveling from one country to another on vacation d) Entering a new country to settle permanently
Matching: Matching items require students to match elements of information that are related. Usually more possible answers are listed than the elements for which they are to be matched.	Match each part of the human brain to its basic function: Frontal lobe — Vision Occipital lobe — Coordination Temporal lobe — Pain Parietal lobe — Touch Memory Balance
Alternative Choice: Alternative-choice items are like multiple choice but they offer only two possible alternative answers.	"Sally sold seashells" is an example of: • Hyperbole • Alliteration

True or False: True-false items require students to determine if a statement is accurate or inaccurate.	Put a check next to each statement that is true about Colorado. 1. Colorado became a state after the Civil War. 2. Colorado is one of the three least populated states. 3. The Rocky Mountains run through Colorado.
Multiple Response: Multiple response items are like multiple-choice items, but more than one alternative is correct. These items should be used only when it is clear that the item includes multiple correct alternatives.	Put a check next to the shapes for which you can find a volume: Circle ____ Cube ____ Sphere ____ Prism ____ Pentagon ____
Fill in the Blank: Although these items technically do not require students to select from a list of alternatives, they are more like selected-response items than short constructed-response items because the answer is so short and so focused.	A fraction in which the numerator is greater than the denominator is a(n) _____.

Selected-response items are usually employed with score 2.0 content simply because that content involves specific vocabulary, details, and basic processes that have straightforward answers and outcomes. Michael C. Rodriguez and Thomas M. Haladyna (2013) offer guidelines for designing selected-response items; these are depicted in table 2.2.

Table 2.2: Guidelines for Selected-Response Items

Feature	Guideline
Content Concerns	• Base each item on one type of content and cognitive demand. • Use new material to elicit higher-level thinking. • Keep the content of items independent of one another. • Avoid overly specific and overly general content. • Avoid opinions unless qualified. • Avoid trick items.
Formatting Concerns	• Format each item vertically instead of horizontally.
Style Concerns	• Edit and proof items. • Keep linguistic complexity appropriate for the group being tested. • Minimize the amount of reading in each item. Avoid window dressing.

Feature	Guideline
Stem Writing	State the central idea in the stem very clearly and concisely. Avoid repetitious wording. Word the stem positively, and avoid negatives, such as *not* or *except*.
Options Writing	• Use only options that are plausible and discriminating. Three options are usually sufficient. • Make sure that only one of these options is the right answer. • Vary the location of the right answer. • Place options in logical or numerical order. • Keep the content of options independent; options should not be overlapping. • Avoid using *none of the above*, *all of the above*, or *I don't know*. • Word the options positively; avoid negatives, such as *not* or *except*. • Avoid giving clues to the answer. • Keep the length of options about equal. • Avoid specific determiners including *always*, *never*, *completely*, and *absolutely*. • Avoid slang associations and options identical to or resembling words in the stem. • Avoid pairs or triplets of options that clue the test taker to the correct choice. • Avoid blatantly absurd, ridiculous options. • Keep options homogeneous in content and grammatical structure. • Make all distractors plausible. Use typical errors of students to write your distractors. • Avoid humorous options.

Source: Rodriguez & Haladyna, 2013.

Designing Short Constructed-Response Items

Constructed-response items span a wide range of formats. According to Thomas P. Hogan (2013), many sources make a dichotomous distinction between selected-response items and constructed response: "The terminology, however, is not universal. Even when these terms are used, what gets classified into each category is not always the same from one source to another" (p. 275).

Hogan (2013) makes a distinction between short-answer items and brief written-response items. I classify them both as short constructed-response items commonly used in traditional tests. The feature that ties these two together—other than students having to generate the content for the answer and express it using connected prose—is that they are focused enough to be found on a single assessment that might also include selected-response items.

It is important to note that short constructed-response items can also include demonstrations that students can execute skills. Hogan (2013) provides examples like the following:

- Using a protractor, bisect this line segment.
- Write an equation to show how to get the perimeter of a rectangle 2 cm wide by 4 cm long.
- Draw a map of your state and locate your city on the map. (p. 279)

While teachers commonly use short constructed-response items for score 2.0 content, teachers also use them for score 3.0 and 4.0 content.

Traditional tests usually require some type of format-specific score that is then translated to a proficiency scale score. Next, I describe scoring assessments that use both selected-response and constructed-response items.

Scoring Assessments That Use Selected-Response and Short Constructed-Response Items

In a series of works, I have described different methods for translating a format-specific score into a proficiency scale score (Marzano, 2006, 2010; Marzano et al., 2017). My general recommendation is that such tests have three sections: (1) one section with items focusing on score 2.0, (2) another section with items focusing on score 3.0, and (3) another with items focusing on score 4.0.

To illustrate, assume a teacher is designing an assessment for a topic related to the angles of triangles. He first creates a proficiency scale. At the score 2.0 level, the proficiency scale includes statements like the following.

Students will be able to recognize and recall basic vocabulary terms, such as *interior angle, exterior angle, angle sum, corresponding angles, congruent,* and *similarity.*

Students will be able to recognize and recall basic facts, such as the measures of the interior angles of a triangle add up to 180 degrees and when two corresponding angles of two triangles are congruent, the triangles are similar.

For the 3.0 content, the proficiency scale includes the following statement.

Students will be able to use evidence to informally explain relationships among the angles of triangles, including the sum of interior angles and angle-angle similarity.

For the score 4.0 content, the proficiency scale includes the following.

Students will be able to compare the angle sum of triangles to those of other polygons.

When designing tests that address all three levels of content, the teacher uses this proficiency scale to construct items. For the 2.0 content, the teacher might design five items with formats like the following in section A of the test.

1. Choose the best answer from the following options.
    When two triangles are congruent:

    A. They have the same interior and exterior sum

    B. One has an area twice as large as the other

    C. They tessellate

    D. Their corresponding sides and angles have the same length and measure

2. Fill in the blank.
    The measures of interior angles of a triangle always add up to _____

3. Draw lines between the corresponding angles of the following triangles.

For section B of the test on score 3.0 content, the teacher might construct three items like the following.

Determine the unknown angle measure in the following triangle. Explain how you know. 52° 90°

In section C of the test that addresses score 4.0 content, the teacher might design two items like the following.

Use the following diagram to determine the angle sum of a convex quadrilateral. Explain your thought process.

Following this pattern, the teacher would have a ten-item test that covers score 2.0, 3.0, and 4.0 content. Ways to score a test like this and translate the format-specific score into a proficiency score include using percentage scores and response codes and addressing aberrant patterns.

Using Percentage Scores

Using percentage scores involves determining what percentage of available points a student earned on each section of a test and using those percentages to assign an appropriate proficiency scale score. Consider figure 2.1.

Section	Item Number	Possible Points per Item	Points Obtained per Item	Section Percentage
Score 2.0	1	5	5	22/25 = 88 percent
	2	5	4	
	3	5	3	
	4	5	5	
	5	5	5	
	Total	25	22	
Score 3.0	6	10	7	15/30 = 50 percent
	7	10	4	
	8	10	4	
	Total	30	15	
Score 4.0	9	10	1	3/20 = 15 percent
	10	10	2	
	Total	20	3	

Source: Adapted from Marzano, Heflebower, Hoegh, Warrick, & Grift, 2016, p. 56.

Figure 2.1: The percentage approach to scoring assessments.

In figure 2.1, there were twenty-five points available in the five items at the score 2.0 level, and the student earned twenty-two of those points. This ratio is converted into a percentage, which is 88 percent. Assuming the teacher set a cut score of 80 percent for this section, it would indicate that the student demonstrates competence with the score 2.0 content. The student also earned 50 percent of the available points in the score 3.0 section, indicating that he or she knows only about half of that content. Based on this evidence, the teacher would likely assign a proficiency scale score of 2.5 for the entire test, indicating no major errors or omissions with the basic content and partial success with the target content.

Using Response Codes

In this method, the teacher marks a student's responses to each item correct (C), partially correct (PC), or incorrect (I) and then examines the pattern of responses to determine the student's proficiency level. Some high school teachers prefer to use codes of low partial (LP) and high partial (HP). To illustrate, consider figure 2.2 (page 46).

In figure 2.2, the student provided correct responses for all five score 2.0 items. The overall score for the 2.0 content was correct. He then provided one correct answer and two partially correct answers, leading to a section 3.0 score of partially correct. Both items in the score 4.0 section were marked incorrect. Because these patterns indicate complete understanding of score 2.0 and partial understanding of score 3.0, this student would receive an overall score of 2.5.

Section	Item Number	Correct, Partially Correct, or Incorrect?	Section Pattern
A Score 2.0	1	C	Correct
	2	C	
	3	C	
	4	C	
	5	C	
B Score 3.0	6	PC	Partially Correct
	7	C	
	8	PC	
C Score 4.0	9	I	Incorrect
	10	I	
Overall Score			2.5

Source: Adapted from Marzano, 2010.

Figure 2.2: The response codes approach to scoring assessments.

Addressing Aberrant Patterns

One question that commonly comes up relative to scoring traditional tests is how to handle student response patterns that are aberrant—patterns that don't seem to make much sense. For example, assume that a student misses several of the score 2.0 items but answers correctly all of the score 3.0 items. One possible reason for such a pattern is that the items don't exhibit content validity in the sense that they don't match the level of difficulty articulated in the scale. For example, it is not always the case that selected-response items measure easier content like that in the score 2.0 section of a scale. In designing a traditional test, a teacher might inadvertently design some selected-response items that more appropriately fit as score 3.0 content. A clue that this has happened would be that many of the students missed the same score 2.0 items. In this case, the teacher could either reclassify the items in terms of their level on the proficiency scale or simply drop them from the test.

Another possibility for an aberrant pattern is that a student was careless with answering the score 2.0 items. If the teacher suspects this, then students can be asked to explain in writing why they missed the simpler items and provide an explanation of the correct answers before assigning a final score.

Still another possibility is that the proficiency score itself is faulty and contains content at the score 2.0 level that is actually more appropriate at the score 3.0 level. I typically recommend that educators revise proficiency scales as needed at the end of each year to accommodate feedback from student responses to assessments.

Essays

Essays were one of the first forms of assessment in schools (Durm, 1993). Hogan (2013) places essays in the category of brief written assignments along with other types of short-constructed response tasks. I believe they should be classified as a unique type of task. Essays stand alone, whereas short constructed-response items are embedded in traditional tests that also include selected-response items. While essays are certainly related to short constructed-response items, they typically provide students much more structure. To illustrate, consider figure 2.3, an example of an essay assessment that might be from a high school social studies course on influential events in U.S. history.

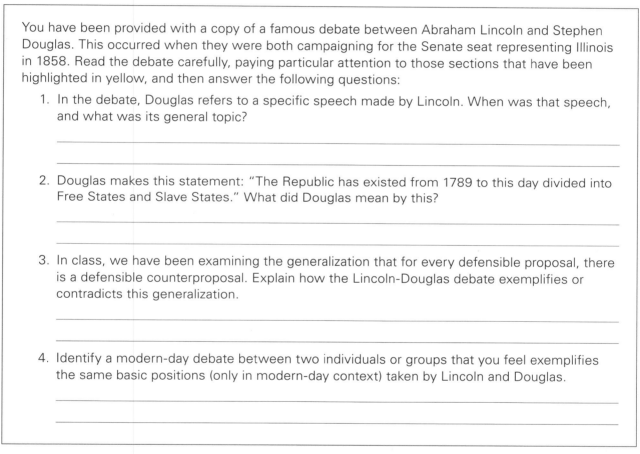

You have been provided with a copy of a famous debate between Abraham Lincoln and Stephen Douglas. This occurred when they were both campaigning for the Senate seat representing Illinois in 1858. Read the debate carefully, paying particular attention to those sections that have been highlighted in yellow, and then answer the following questions:

1. In the debate, Douglas refers to a specific speech made by Lincoln. When was that speech, and what was its general topic?

2. Douglas makes this statement: "The Republic has existed from 1789 to this day divided into Free States and Slave States." What did Douglas mean by this?

3. In class, we have been examining the generalization that for every defensible proposal, there is a defensible counterproposal. Explain how the Lincoln-Douglas debate exemplifies or contradicts this generalization.

4. Identify a modern-day debate between two individuals or groups that you feel exemplifies the same basic positions (only in modern-day context) taken by Lincoln and Douglas.

Figure 2.3: An example of an essay assessment.

This essay assessment design might emerge from a specific proficiency scale that focused on a measurement topic titled The Influence of Political Events. The score 2.0 content on the proficiency scale might contain specific information about particular political events like the Lincoln-Douglas debate. The score 3.0 content might contain generalizations about the effects of political events: "For every defensible proposal, there is a defensible counterproposal." The score 4.0 content might require students to link past and current events. From the perspective of such a scale, the first two questions in the essay task address score 2.0 content, the third question addresses score 3.0 content, and the fourth question addresses score 4.0 content.

Obviously, once you design essays, you must consider how you will score them. Teachers can score essays designed to encompass score 2.0, 3.0, and 4.0 content from a proficiency scale in a manner similar to the traditional test. In this case, teachers would analyze the score 2.0 items separately, and the same with the score 3.0 and score 4.0 items. It's best to start with the score 2.0 items—items 1 and 2—and establish a point system for each item. Let's say five points are assigned to item 1 and item 2, which would mean that score 2.0 content involves ten points. A teacher would establish a cut score, indicating that a student provided sufficient evidence to warrant the assignment of a 2.0. For example, a teacher might establish a cut score of 8 out of 10 as the criterion for receiving a score or 2.0. If the student achieved this cut score, the teacher would score item 3, which deals with score 3.0 content. Again, the teacher would assign a certain number of points to item 3 and a cut score that relates to those points. The teacher would apply the same process to item 4, which addresses the score 4.0 content. The teacher would examine the pattern of responses across the three categories and assign an overall score for the assessment.

Aberrant patterns would be addressed in the same manner as before. Score 2.0 questions might not have been worded well, causing some students who knew the target content to receive low scores on these items. Realizing this, the teacher might lower the cut score or ask some students to briefly restate their answers orally or in writing before assigning a grade.

Instead of points, a teacher might also use the response coding system in which items are coded as I (incorrect), C (correct), LP (low partial), or HP (high partial). Both the point system and the response code system would be considered format-specific scores that translate into scores on the proficiency scale. Again, this is the essence of the measurement process.

Performance Tasks, Demonstrations, and Presentations

According to Suzanne Lane (2013), the measurement community has positively viewed performance assessments for quite some time. Literature has cited them frequently, and they are thought to possess qualities that go beyond the confines of traditional assessments. In the 1999 and 2014 editions of *The Standards for Educational and Psychological Testing* (AERA et al., 1999, 2014), performance assessments involve products and behaviors designed to emulate real-life contexts in which specific knowledge and skills are actually applied.

Lane (2013) notes that educators seem to have a natural affinity for performance assessments for at least three reasons: (1) they allow for demonstrations of knowledge and skills that cannot easily be assessed with other formats, (2) they serve as exemplars of the types of tasks that stimulate and enrich learning as opposed to demonstrations of learning only, and (3) they help shape sound instructional practices by modeling what is important to learn and how it might best be taught. For these reasons, Lane (2013) notes, "These qualities make performance assessments ideal tools for formative, interim, and summative assessments that can be naturally embedded in instruction" (p. 313).

In several writings, I have identified specific types of tasks that would qualify as acceptable performance tasks (Marzano, 1992, 2017; Marzano & Kendall, 2007, 2008). I briefly describe them in table 2.3.

Table 2.3: Types of Performance Tasks

Performance Task	Description	Example
Decision Making	Decision making involves selecting among alternatives.	Your job is to determine who among the following individuals would be the best peacetime leader out of the following: (a) Martin Luther King, Jr., (b) Franklin Roosevelt, or (c) Barack Obama.
Problem Solving	Problem solving involves accomplishing a goal for which an obstacle or limiting condition exists.	Your job is to build a fence that encompasses the largest area with 1,000 feet of two-by-four-inch planks. You must perform all computations and estimations mentally. You may not use a calculator or keep track of your calculations using a pencil or paper. Explain how the use of estimation and mental computation affected your ability to solve this problem.
Experimental Inquiry	Experimental inquiry involves the generation and testing of hypotheses about a specific physical or psychological phenomenon.	We have been studying principles concerning how human beings react to certain types of information. Select one of these principles and make a prediction about how students your age would react to a specific type of advertisement. Be sure to explain the logic behind your predictions. Carry out an activity to test your prediction, and explain whether the results confirm or disprove your original hypothesis.
Historical Investigation	Historical investigation involves examining a past event for which different opinions or data exist. Students analyze opinions and data. Students take a position that is supported by evidence.	We have been studying the 1963 assassination of John F. Kennedy. There are many conflicting accounts. Identify one of the conflicting accounts of this incident, and investigate what is known about it. Defend a position on this issue.
Projective Investigation	Projective investigation involves examining a possible future event for which different opinions or data exist. Students analyze opinions and data. Based on their analyses, they take a position and then support it with evidence.	We have been studying the relationship between the temperature of the oceans and polar ice caps. Using your knowledge of these principles, investigate what might happen if the earth's temperature were to rise by five degrees over the next three decades.

Performance Task	Description	Example
Definitional Investigation	Definitional investigation involves examining a concept for which different opinions or data exist. Students analyze opinions and data. Based on their analyses, they take a position and then support with evidence.	Legislation in this state protects *old-growth forests* (defined as one that has been around for a long time without any significant disturbance). However, definitions of old-growth forests differ. Identify differing opinions about the defining characteristics of an old-growth forest. Take and defend a position on this issue.

Source: Adapted from Marzano & Kendall, 1996.

Performance tasks commonly contain embedded demonstrations and presentations. Technically, demonstrations and presentations include some important differences. The term *demonstration* implies some confirmation or verification of a certain level of knowledge. Therefore, students probably best apply demonstrations to skills and processes. For example, a student could provide a demonstration of his ability to solve inequalities, or a student could provide a demonstration regarding her ability to make and defend a complex decision.

The term *presentation* strongly implies an audience of some sort, whereas the term *demonstration* does not. Therefore, a student could engage in a demonstration viewed by a single person (such as a teacher) that does not involve much presentation. A presentation, by definition, involves a broader audience than a teacher. Noting this, presentations do not have to be live; a student could record a presentation that might be viewed only by the teacher. However, the student should adhere to all the general guidelines for making a formal presentation, such as using a well-structured beginning, middle, and ending; looking at the audience or camera; speaking clearly; and so on.

When scoring performance tasks, demonstrations, and presentations, a teacher should follow the same guidelines as those for essays. If the teacher designs the task to include levels 2.0, 3.0, and 4.0 of a proficiency scale, then the teacher must provide specific directions to the students as to how they must illustrate their knowledge for these content levels. In effect, then, the directions for these tasks are very similar to the directions for essays.

This category of assessments contains some built-in traps teachers should look out for. They all commonly include multiple dimensions. For example, consider a presentation in which students must illustrate their ability to conduct a historical investigation. This task would include the actual content of the investigation, but it would also include presentation skills. In this case, two scores must be assigned: (1) content and (2) presentation ability. The ability to make effective presentations would have its own proficiency scale, as would the content that is the focus of the investigation.

Portfolios

According to the 1999 and the 2014 editions of *The Standards for Educational and Psychological Testing* (AERA et al., 1999, 2014), portfolios, when used for assessments, are systematic collections of educational products compiled or accumulated over time according to a specific set of principles. Susan F. Belgrad (2013) explains that portfolios were first implemented during the 1970s in progressive schools. They were thrust into the public eye of educators in the National Writing Project as a substitute for a written exit exam in 1983 and "became widely used in K–12 classrooms in the 1990s, largely in response to renewed efforts to engage and educate all children through student-centered curriculum and instruction" (Belgrad, 2013, p. 331).

Belgrad (2013) notes that one of the biggest problems with portfolios is standardizing their scoring. I agree, and I go one step further in my assertion that it is better to think of portfolios as collections of evidence for competence in several measurement topics (as opposed to a single topic). For example, students might be in a social studies class that involves five measurement topics during a specific grading period. The students might be asked to keep a portfolio of their performance in these topics as evidence of their overall competence across the topics. To this extent, then, teachers do not score these portfolios, per se, since they contain the artifacts for measurement topics that have already been scored. A teacher could judge the cumulative evidence provided in a portfolio as so compelling that summative scores on measurement topics could be raised.

Probing Discussions

One of the most flexible types of assessment is probing discussions. This type involves the teacher sitting down with a student with a proficiency scale in hand and asking a series of questions. The impetus for this type of assessment came from a study conducted by Sheila Valencia and her colleagues (Valencia, Stallman, Commeyras, Pearson, & Hartman, 1991). They assessed students' knowledge of a specific topic in four ways: (1) a fill-in-the-blank test, (2) a short-answer test, (3) an essay, and (4) a structured discussion. The structured discussion provided the most information about students regarding the topic of assessment. The researchers note, "On average, 66% of the topically relevant ideas students gave during interviews were not tested on . . . [other] measures" (Valencia et al., 1991, p. 226). In other words, the other types of assessment provided only 34 percent of the information that the structured discussion could have provided.

Over the years, I have referred to structured discussions as *probing discussions*. To conduct a probing discussion, the teacher interacts with a specific student for about three to five minutes. The teacher asks question about score 2.0, 3.0, and 4.0 content. One of the nice features about such discussions is that the teacher can go back to previously posed questions and ask students to clarify or elaborate on their original answers.

Of course, once you've had your probing discussions, you'll need to consider scoring them. When scoring probing discussions, the teacher typically starts with score 2.0 content and continues until he or she is convinced that the student's score is at least a 2.0. When the teacher believes that the student will receive a solid 2.0, the teacher then moves to the 3.0 content and asks questions until convinced the student has achieved this status, and so on. Even if a student doesn't demonstrate strong score 2.0 knowledge, the teacher might still move on to some 3.0 content. If the student appears strong on this more advanced content, the teacher might consider the student's responses to the easier content as an aberrant pattern and then give the student more opportunities to demonstrate score 2.0 content.

Probing discussions usually don't involve any format-specific score. Rather, the teacher engages students in a discussion and then directly translates the results of that discussion into a score on the proficiency scale.

Student Self-Assessments

In 2009, John Hattie published his synthesis of the findings of over eight hundred meta-analyses relating to student achievement in the book *Visible Learning*. There, he ranked 138 variables in terms of their effect sizes when student achievement was the dependent variable. Hattie (2009) describes the term *effect size* in depth as well—an effect size quantifies the strength of the relationship between two variables. In Hattie's (2009) study, the dependent variable was always student achievement, and the independent variables were typical interventions schools have employed for decades (like class size, homework, practice, questioning techniques, and so on). Of the 138 variables Hattie examined, student self-reported grades was rated the highest with an effect size of 1.44. Taken at face value, this implies that students might see more than a forty-percentile-point gain in achievement when they engage in this activity.

In 2012, in *Visible Learning for Teachers* Hattie updated his review of the research and added twelve new variables for a grand total of 150. Student self-reported grades was still ranked first, but he expanded his discussion of the concept, emphasizing that it involves a number of interacting components. In 2009, Hattie defined it as students being aware of their current levels of performance and making predictions about their future performance. He notes:

> Students were very knowledgeable about their chances of success. On the one hand, this shows a remarkably high level of predictability about achievement in the classroom (and should question the necessity of so many tests when students appear to already have much of the information the tests supposedly provide), but on the other hand, these expectations of success (which are sometimes set lower than students could attain) may become a barrier for some students as they may only perform to whatever expectations they already have of their ability. (Hattie, 2009, p. 44)

Hattie (2012) summarizes his overall findings, saying, "Educating students to have high, challenging, appropriate expectations is among the most powerful influence in enhancing student achievement" (p. 60). From these comments, one might infer that Hattie's highest-ranking strategy is a combination of student self-analysis, coupled with the student setting of personal goals for academic content that are both attainable and challenging. Marzano et al. (2017) propose the use of the personal tracking matrix as one way of accomplishing this goal.

A personal tracking matrix is akin to a capacity matrix, developed by David P. Langford (2015), to support individuals in charting their own learning toward a specific result. Teachers design personal tracking matrices right from proficiency scales. Consider figure 2.4.

4.0	The student will: • Test the idea that solving linear equations by graphing is the best solution method for particular situations. For example, list situations in which solving by graphing is the most efficient solution method and situations in which solving algebraically is the most efficient solution method.
3.5	In addition to score 3.0 performance, partial success at score 4.0 content
3.0	The student will: • Solve linear equations by graphing. For example, find the point that will satisfy two linear equations by graphing both equations.
2.5	No major errors or omissions regarding score 2.0 content, and partial success at score 3.0 content

2.0	The student will:
	• Recognize or recall specific vocabulary—for example, *linear equation*, *slope-intercept form*, *coordinate plane*, and *intersection point*—and perform basic processes, such as:
	    ◆ Convert a linear equation into slope-intercept form
	    ◆ Graph a linear equation on a coordinate plane
	    ◆ Determine the intersection point for the graphs of two linear equations
	    ◆ Verify the point of intersection by inserting the coordinates into each linear equation

1.5	Partial success at score 2.0 content, and major errors or omissions regarding score 3.0 content
1.0	With help, partial success at score 2.0 content and score 3.0 content
0.5	With help, partial success at score 2.0 content but not at score 3.0 content
0.0	Even with help, no success

Figure 2.4: Proficiency scale for solving linear equations through graphing.

Figure 2.4 contains a proficiency scale for the high school measurement topic of solving linear equations through graphing. Teachers can transform it into a personal tracking matrix by rephrasing the content. This is depicted in figure 2.5 (page 54).

The personal tracking matrix in figure 2.5 rewrites each learning target in the proficiency scale into an *I can* format. The personal tracking matrix also breaks some elements into more detail. For example, the personal tracking matrix gives each vocabulary term its own line for rating. It also contains sections for students to rate themselves and list evidence for their ratings. That scale has three levels: (1) I'm still confused about this topic, (2) I've learned some but not all of this topic, and (3) I've got this now.

Note that on the personal tracking matrix, the student has indicated that she is competent on most of the score 2.0 content since she has noted *I've got this now* on all but two elements. The evidence the student listed includes online practice activities the teacher had provided and practice activities in centers the teacher had set up.

Level	Indicator	My Rating			My Evidence
		I'm still confused about this topic.	I've learned some but not all of the topic.	I've got this now.	
4	I can show situations in which solving a linear equation is best done through graphing versus situations in which it is best done algebraically.	x			Practice activity 4
3	I can find the point that will satisfy two linear equations by graphing both equations.	x	x		Practice activity 3
2	I can verify the point of intersection by inserting the coordinates into each linear equation.	x	x		Practice activity 3
2	I can determine the intersection point of the graphs of two linear equations.	x	x	x	Practice activity 2
2	I can graph a linear equation on a coordinate plane.	x	x		Practice activity 2
2	I can convert a linear equation into its slope-intercept form.	x	x	x	Practice activity 1
2	I can provide an explanation of the term *intersection point*.	x	x	x	Online exercise 1 and 2
2	I can provide an explanation of the term *coordinate plane*.	x	x	x	Online exercise 1 and 2
2	I can provide an explanation of the term *slope-intercept form*.	x	x	x	Online exercise 1 and 2
2	I can provide an explanation of the term *linear equation*.	x	x	x	Online exercise 1 and 2

Figure 2.5: Personal tracking matrix for solving linear equations through graphing.

Scoring student self-assessments commonly requires a student to provide additional information the teacher requested. For the teacher to use the personal tracking matrix as an assessment, he or she might ask the student to provide more evidence for the assigned scores rather than that already listed in the tracking matrix. This extra evidence might come in the form of a portfolio the student keeps with related assignments and assessments or evidence that has been archived electronically. The teacher would examine the student's self-assessment (represented in the personal tracking matrix) and the supporting evidence and translate it into a score on the proficiency scale. After the teacher's analysis of the personal tracking matrix, the teacher usually has a brief conversation with the student. While interacting with the student, the teacher might decide that the student's self-assessment warrants a score of 2.0 on the proficiency scale, even though the student assigned himself a score of 2.5.

In addition to using the personal tracking matrix to assign scores on the proficiency scale, the teacher would ensure that students set goals of what they will work on next. Recall that Hattie's (2012) construct of self-reported grades and student expectations involves both assessing one's current status and setting challenging but attainable short-term goals.

Assessments That Cover One Level of a Proficiency Scale

Teachers frequently use all the previously described assessments to evaluate all content levels of a proficiency scale. Teachers more commonly use some types of assessments for specific proficiency scale levels, although the teachers can design all of these to include the whole scale. Topics involved here include voting techniques, observations, and student-generated assessments.

Voting Techniques

Many teachers utilize electronically based voting techniques. There are many free websites that allow teachers to do this, such as Kahoot! (https://getkahoot.com), Quizzizz (https://quizzizz.com), and Socrative (https://socrative.com). While teachers frequently use voting techniques to obtain a general sense of how the class as a whole is doing, they can also use them to record scores for individual students on specific levels of content in a proficiency scale. This is particularly the case for score 2.0 content that involves details and basic processes. To do so, the teacher might create selected-response items for the content—say five items—to use during a class period. The teacher then asks the class to answer the items at the end of the period. The teacher might go over the answers with students but then use the scores for each individual student recorded before the class discusses the answers as evidence of their current status on the score 2.0 content. The teacher would establish some cut score like *at least four items correct* as the criterion for assigning a score of 2.0. If a student gets three items correct, the teacher might record a score of 1.5 or 1.75.

Next, observations involve the teacher noticing a student demonstrating a specific level of proficiency and recording a score.

Observations

Score 2.0 content that involves skills, strategies, and processes are most often the subject of observations. For example, a teacher might observe a student using a piece of information in a class discussion that represents score 2.0 content on a scale and record that score. However, a teacher might also observe evidence of score 3.0 content. For example, a language arts teacher might notice a student independently executing the correct procedures for ensuring that an essay features good transitions from paragraph to paragraph. Teachers score observations directly onto a proficiency scale. They typically do not involve format-specific scores.

Student-Generated Assessments

Although teachers could use student-generated assessments for all three levels of a proficiency scale, they are more commonly applied to a specific level. This occurs when a student believes he or she has attained a specific score on a proficiency scale but simply has not shown it on any teacher-initiated assessments. In such cases, the student comes to the teacher and describes how she will submit evidence for proficiency at a specific level. This commonly occurs at the score 3.0 and 4.0 levels. To illustrate, assume that a particular student has not yet demonstrated score 3.0 status on the topic of solving linear equations through graphing, depicted in figure 2.4 (page 53). In that proficiency scale, score 3.0 means that the student must find the point that will satisfy two linear equations by graphing both equations. While the student might not have demonstrated this on a teacher-designed assessment, the student would design her own assessment in which she provides a graph of two intersecting linear functions and submit a video containing her explanation of how the graphs demonstrate the solution.

The Complete Measurement Process

As previously described, teachers can use a wide variety of assessments. This now completes the picture of the measurement process introduced in figure 1.6 (page 37) in chapter 1. Consider figure 2.6, where the top box now includes the various types of assessments teachers can use to gather information about a student's current status on a particular proficiency scale. Teachers translate the format-specific scores derived from these types of assessment to scores on the 0.0 to 4.0 proficiency scale and then record them for the specific proficiency scale to which they relate.

Next, I will delve into the topic of assessment planning.

Assessment Planning

When teachers use proficiency scales, planning for assessments looks very different from what occurs in the traditional classroom. In the traditional system—in which proficiency scales are not employed—the emphasis in planning starts with a general consideration of the number and types of formal assessments that will be used. These types commonly include a midterm and final exam. They also include a fair number of quizzes. Other than this global planning, teachers design these individual assessments independently and situationally. While the teacher will certainly have a general idea of the content in each test, there is little systematic consideration as to the item's difficulty level. The teacher simply designs items focused on the topics they have addressed during a set of lessons and assigns points to the items.

Also, there is little or no consideration about keeping assessments unidimensional. To score the tests, the teacher simply adds the points a student receives and divides by the total possible points. He or she then translates it into a percentage score and records it in a gradebook.

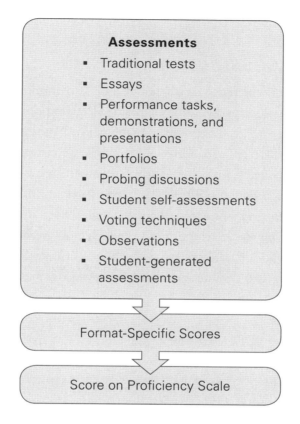

Assessments

- Traditional tests
- Essays
- Performance tasks, demonstrations, and presentations
- Portfolios
- Probing discussions
- Student self-assessments
- Voting techniques
- Observations
- Student-generated assessments

Format-Specific Scores

Score on Proficiency Scale

Figure 2.6: The complete measurement process.

In a classroom where CAs are based on proficiency scales, there is a great deal of structure in place for planning assessments for each measurement topic. My strong recommendation is that teachers plan a comprehensive pretest and posttest for each measurement topic. This means that an adequate number of different items are designed to address score 2.0, 3.0, and 4.0 content on two separate tests.

A unit of instruction usually begins with a teacher administering a pretest to the entire class; however, a teacher could administer it to individual students as they become ready to address a specific measurement topic. The teacher might also administer the posttest to the entire class or administer it to individual students when they are ready to demonstrate proficiency (score 3.0 or higher).

In between the pre- and post-assessments, the teacher uses assessments as opportunities present themselves and as needs arise. It is important to note that these assessments will be with individual students for the most part. For example, during a single class period, the teacher might have probing discussions with some students in the class and record their scores. Additionally, the teacher might observe a few students who clearly demonstrate a particular level of proficiency on the scale. It might also be the case that some students prepare student-generated assessments for particular levels of proficiency on the scale. Finally, a teacher might seek out students who do not have much recorded assessment data for a specific measurement topic. The teacher might have a brief probing discussion with these students and then record the scores for these assessments. In effect, while students are working independently or in small groups, the teacher is circulating about the classroom collecting assessment data as part of the measurement process.

Differentiated Assessments

Much has been written about differentiated instruction. Carol Ann Tomlinson and Tonya R. Moon (2013) explain that effective differentiation involves five elements: (1) classroom environment, (2) curriculum, (3) assessment, (4) instruction, and (5) classroom management. Of these, assessment has received very little attention. By definition, differentiated CA would involve determining students' academic needs, setting goals that address these needs, and then using assessment to maintain progress. The new paradigms for CAs fit these requirements quite well. If teachers use a proficiency scale to establish each student's initial status on a measurement topic, then they can design and administer assessments that fit each student's current status on the continuum of knowledge. As we have seen, these assessments can be probing discussions, observations, and other relatively brief interactions with individual students. I believe that proficiency scales and the measurement processes described in this book can make differentiated CA a reality.

Summary

This chapter addresses the various types of assessments available to teachers as they design CAs. They include traditional tests, essays, performance tasks, demonstrations, presentations, portfolios, probing discussions, student self-assessments, voting techniques, observations, and student-generated assessments. Each of these can be enhanced by the content specificity of proficiency scales, making the construction of parallel assessments a relatively straightforward task for teachers. This array of assessments rounds out the picture of the measurement process in which assessments of all types provide evidence teachers use to assign scores on proficiency scales. The expanded view of the measurement process also sheds light on how differentiated assessment might manifest in the classroom.

Next, I'll discuss the CA paradigm for reliability.

chapter 3

Discussing the CA Paradigm for Reliability

As mentioned in the introduction, the view of reliability from the CA perspective represents a dramatic shift in measurement theory, because it is based on determining score precisions for individual students as measured over a set of parallel assessments as opposed to the differences between students' scores on a single test. What is perhaps most unique and powerful about the new paradigm for reliability is that it involves explicit estimation of each student's true score on each assessment. These estimations account for the possible error in the observed scores. To understand this shift in perspective, it is useful to discuss the traditional view of reliability in some depth. Later in this chapter, I'll also discuss estimating true scores using mathematical models, using technology, discussing the implications for formative and summative scores, using instructional feedback, employing the method of mounting evidence, and considering the issue of scales.

Discussing the Traditional View of Reliability

The traditional view of reliability is based on examining test scores for groups of students. More precisely, the technical definition of reliability is:

> The degree to which test scores of a *group* [emphasis added] of test takers are consistent over repeated applications of a measurement procedure and hence are inferred to be dependable and consistent for an individual test taker; the degree to which scores are free of random errors of measurement for a given group. (AERA et al., 2014, pp. 222-223)

It is useful to note that this is the same technical definition used for the concept of precision (see AERA et al., 2014). The term *reliability*, then, is generally considered synonymous with the term *precision* in the measurement literature. Henceforth, I will use the term *reliability* when discussing the traditional approach, which is based on the large-scale paradigm, but I will use the term *precision* when discussing the new paradigm for CA.

The preceding definition underscores the fact that the classical definition of reliability is grounded in the perspective of scores from a group of test takers. It is also useful to reemphasize the fact that repeated applications of a measurement procedure are central to the traditional concept of reliability. Indeed, Parkes (2013) notes, "Replication is seminal, even definitional, to [measurement] theory" (p. 108).

Now, I'll discuss foundations of the traditional concept of reliability; the concept of error score; the concept of true score; the correlation coefficient and the reliability coefficient; the conceptual formula for reliability; reliability determination using a single test; and the Achilles heel of the reliability coefficient. Understanding these issues provides a concrete foundation for understanding the CA paradigm for reliability.

Foundations of the Traditional Concept of Reliability

What I have been referring to as the large-scale or traditional approach is more appropriately referred to as *classical test theory*. It began with "little more than the idea that an obtained score represents a sample from some larger set that might be obtained instead" (Haertel, 2006, p. 68). By definition, if an observed score is a sample from a larger set, then the observed score must not necessarily be the most accurate or true score for a test taker. As mentioned in the introduction, the basic equation for traditional test theory is observed score = true score + error score.

This equation mathematically represents the simple but foundational notion that an obtained score is a sample from a much larger set and, therefore, contains some error. It is the true score that is the holy grail of assessments. Every assessment is intended to provide evidence as to the true score of each student who takes a test.

Whole traditions of measurement theory have been developed around this simple idea. There are three basic traditions in education and psychological measurement: (1) classical test theory, (2) generalizability theory, and (3) item response theory. Of these, the most germane to this conversation are classical test theory and generalizability theory. (For a more detailed discussion of item response theory, see Marzano, 2006.) Classical test theory explicitly uses the preceding basic equation. Generalizability theory uses the same basic model except that true score is referred to as the *universe score* and multiple aspects of error are considered in the model. Item response theory uses relatively complex mathematical models of true score and error score and combines those models in ways that produce a student's most probable score on a test given his or her pattern of responses. However different, all three approaches operate from the perspective that every score on every test contains errors to one degree or another.

The Concept of Error Score

While the concept of error seems intuitively obvious, it took the world of science quite a while to articulate and accept it formally. According to Ross E. Traub (1997), Galileo in the 17th century was one of the first scientists to formally acknowledge the influence of error on measurement. He noted that errors of observations tended to be distributed systematically and cluster around their true score. By the 18th century, the theory of errors and true scores had become more solidified mathematically. For example, mathematical models were established describing the distributions of random error scores one could expect across a set of scores. By the beginning of the 19th century, the concept of error was well established, with scientists like Carl Friedrich Gauss deriving formulas for the distribution of random error.

The Concept of True Score

Along with better models for the nature of error, the concept of true score became more clearly defined. It was assumed that the amount of error for any given measurement was unpredictable. Therefore, it was referred to as *random error*. However, if enough measurements were taken for a single test taker, the errors would tend to cancel out each other. This is why replication is so important; it allows for the estimation of true scores.

Traub (1997) notes that Gauss attempted to prove "that the mean of many observations of an unknown quantity, such as a parameter of the orbit of a planet, is the most likely value of that quantity" (p. 9). *True score* became defined as the average of multiple measurements of the same person on the same trait with the same type of test or measurement (see Lord & Novick, 1968).

The Correlation Coefficient and the Reliability Coefficient

The development of the correlation coefficient played a major part in the development of the classical test theory. Traub (1997) notes that the term *correlation* was first used in a technical sense in 1888 in the article "Co-relations and Their Measurement" (Galton, 1888). Traub (1997) further explains that credit for referring to the measure of the co-relationship between variables as the *correlation coefficient* belongs to Francis Y. Edgeworth and dates from 1892.

The history of the correlation coefficient is an intriguing one with several differing opinions as to how it should be computed and what it means (see Pearson, 1920). In fact, many indices are referred to as correlations. For our purposes, though, a *correlation coefficient* is a measure of the strength of the relationship between two measures. If the coefficient is close to 0.00, then there is little or no relationship between the measures. If the correlation is close to positive or negative 1.00, then there is a very strong relationship between the two measures.

The correlation coefficient helped set the stage for the development of the reliability coefficient, when Charles Spearman (1904) noted that the correlation between pairs of measurement should help one estimate how much error existed in the measures. If two sets of measurements of the same topic had a high correlation approaching 1.0, then the measures, by definition, had relatively little error. Conversely, if two measures had a low correlation approaching 0.00, then one or both had a great deal of error. The correlation coefficient made it possible to operationalize the reliability coefficient.

Truman L. Kelley (1942) lays out a seminal explanation of the reliability coefficient and its basis in the replication of identical or equivalent tests. Kelley (1942) notes that a "belief that two or more measures of a mental function exist is a prerequisite to the concept of reliability, and further, not only exist but that they are available before a measure of reliability is possible" (p. 76). Gulliksen (1950) states that "we shall define reliability as the correlation between two parallel forms of a test" (p. 13). This conception of the reliability coefficient was straightforward and well accepted. For example, Robert L. Ebel (1951) states that the "process for estimating test reliability by two sets of scores is well known" (p. 407). Edward E. Cureton (1958) notes, "It has been common practice to define the reliability coefficient as the correlation between equivalent forms of a test" (p. 715). Magnusson (1967) states that the "correlation coefficient for the agreement between repeated measures under similar conditions constitutes the numerical value of the reliability of the data which can be obtained with a given instrument" (p. 61).

To illustrate this straightforward approach to the reliability coefficient, reconsider the example provided in table I.1 in the introduction (page 9) and reproduced in table 3.1.

Table 3.1: Three Administrations of the Same Test

	Initial Administration	Second Administration (A)	Second Administration (B)
Student 1	97	98	82
Student 2	92	90	84
Student 3	86	80	79
Student 4	83	83	72
Student 5	81	79	66
Student 6	80	83	70
Student 7	78	78	66
Student 8	77	74	55
Student 9	70	68	88
Student 10	65	66	78
Correlation With Initial Administration		0.96	0.32

As described in table I.1 in the introduction, the column Initial Administration represents the scores of ten students on a test. The column Second Administration (A) represents an administration of the test soon after the first administration under the condition that students forgot about the first administration. As described, the pattern of similarities between the pairs of scores for students indicates a high reliability, but we now have a correlation between scores on these two administrations that quantifies the degree of relationship. That correlation is 0.96 and represents the reliability coefficient under the traditional definition of reliability. As described in the introduction, the pattern of dissimilarities between the pairs of scores in Second Administration (B) and Initial Administration indicates low reliability. We now have the correlation between these two administrations (0.32) that verifies the low reliability. The reliability coefficient obtained by correlating two administrations of the same test to the same students seems to provide a clear and unequivocal index of reliability.

Again, the idea is straightforward. Correlations of multiple administrations of the same test to the same students is an intuitively appealing way to compute reliability. Unfortunately, this approach to computing reliability is difficult, if not impossible, to implement in practice. This changed with work by Louis Guttman (1945).

The Conceptual Formula for Reliability

A major breakthrough in the practice of computing reliability coefficients came from Guttman (1945). Using the basic equation of classical test theory, he proved mathematically that reliability could be defined conceptually as the ratio of the true variance over the observed variance without the need to make limiting assumptions about the nature of the error within each measurement:

> No assumptions of zero means for errors or zero correlations are needed to prove that the total variance of the test is the sum of the error variance and the variance of the expected scores . . . . Therefore, the reliability coefficient is defined without assumptions of independence as the complement of the ratio of error variance to total variance. (Guttman, 1945, p. 257)

This solidified the already popular conceptual definition of reliability as a ratio of variances.

Reliability = true score variance / observed score variance

Roughly speaking, *variance* is a measure of differences in scores on a single assessment. The more scores on a test are different, the greater the variance. (See also basic texts on statistics for a more technical definition; for example, Salkind, 2017.)

The conceptual formula provides a different perspective on reliability than that provided by the correlation between repeated administrations of the same test under the assumption that students remained the same from administration to administration. Rather, the conceptual formula supports the view that a test's reliability can be determined from a single administration if the variance of the true scores could be estimated. Since you can compute the variance of the observed scores directly from the test data, all that is needed to form the ratio explicit in the conceptual formula is an estimate of the true score variance. In this case, there would be no need for repeated administration of the same test.

The Reliability Determination Using a Single Test

Guttman's (1945) contribution helped advance the notion that a test's reliability could be computed from a single administration of a test. This solved the perplexing problem of repeated administrations: "As is well known, there may be great practical difficulties in making two independent trials; therefore, our principal focus is on *what information can be obtained from a single trial*" (Guttman, 1945, p. 257; emphasis in original).

Psychometricians doubled their efforts to construct appropriate formulas to compute reliability from a single test administration. In fact, it is fair to say that this has been test developers' predominant interest for quite a while. As Feldt and Brennan (1993) note, the field of measurement has been preoccupied for years with identifying techniques for computing reliability coefficients from a single test:

> For more than three quarters of a century, measurement theoreticians have been concerned with reliability estimation in the absence of parallel forms. Spearman (1910) and Brown (1910) posed the problem; their solution is incorporated in the well-known formula bearing their names. In the ensuing decades, a voluminous literature has accumulated on this topic. The problem is an intensely practical one. For many tests, only one form is produced, because a second would be rarely needed . . . . Even when parallel forms exist and the trait or skill is not undergoing rapid change, practical considerations might rule out administration of more than one form. (p. 110)

These efforts have led to the development of several formulas for reliability that could be applied to a single assessment. Some of the more well-known formulas were Spearman-Brown, KR20, KR21, and probably the most widely used reliability formula, Cronbach's coefficient alpha. The names of these formulas provide no insight into their nature. In fact, many reliability formulas are named after their designers. A simple Internet search will provide the formulas for each. The important point for this discussion is that they are all techniques for computing the reliability for an assessment from a single administration under the assumption that reliability is the ratio of the true score variance to the observed score variance.

The Achilles Heel of the Reliability Coefficient

From the previous discussions, it is easy to conclude that over some one hundred years, the reliability coefficient has been an unquestioned staple of test development. This is unfortunate, especially for CAs. One of the major reasons is that reliability coefficients designed for single test administrations are not designed to make instructional decisions about individual students. Indeed, Cronbach notes, "I doubt whether coefficient alpha is the best way of judging the reliability of the instrument to which it is applied" (Cronbach & Shavelson, 2004, p. 393). He further explains that reliability coefficients in general tell us little about the scores of individual students: "Coefficients are a crude device that does not bring to the surface many subtleties implied by variance components" (Cronbach & Shavelson, 2004, p. 394).

The major weakness of the reliability coefficient from the perspective of a teacher trying to interpret students' scores on a CA was depicted in the introduction. There we saw that to interpret an individual student's observed score, a confidence interval can be computed for each score. Reconsider the 95 percent confidence intervals for an observed score of 75 as depicted in table I.2 (page 11) in the introduction. An observed score of 75 has a 95 percent confidence interval of 69 to 81 even when the reliability of the test is as high as 0.85. That confidence interval expands to 64 to 86 when the test's reliability is 0.55. Additionally, while the 95 percent confidence interval tells us the range of scores in which the true score most probably falls, it doesn't provide any mathematical estimate of the true score other than the observed score itself.

Estimating True Scores Using Mathematical Models

Clearly, if classroom teachers are to be held accountable for designing assessments that produce precise scores, a new paradigm for reliability must be used. As highlighted in the introduction, this new paradigm focuses on the precision of the scores of individual students over time. Recall that I am using the term *precision* here to distinguish this process from that applied to the reliability of score sets on a single assessment. Also recall that in the measurement literature, the terms *reliability* and *precision* have the same meaning (AERA et al., 2014).

The validity prerequisites for the new precision paradigm are outlined in chapter 2 (page 39) and in this chapter. Educators should identify measurement topics articulated as proficiency scales from which they design and administer parallel assessments to students. Teachers translate the results of these parallel assessments to scores on the appropriate proficiency scale via the measurement process. This process results in a series of scores on the same topic for each student that are directly comparable. The teachers then analyze these scores to estimate students' true scores.

The most rigorous way to estimate the true scores for individual students across a series of parallel assessments is to use the mathematical models in this section. Educators can construct an Excel spreadsheet using the formulas in technical notes 3.1, 3.2, and 3.3 (page 111). I discuss the spreadsheet's design and use later in this chapter. I have found that those who are experienced with Excel can use these formulas quite readily, albeit with great attention to detail. In addition, the resource designed by Haystead and Marzano (2017) provides specific guidance in Excel programming. Finally, if there is no one available who can carry out Excel programming, teachers can always use the method of mounting evidence (page 74), but the method of mathematical models is certainly the more precise. To understand the use of mathematical models, see figure 3.1.

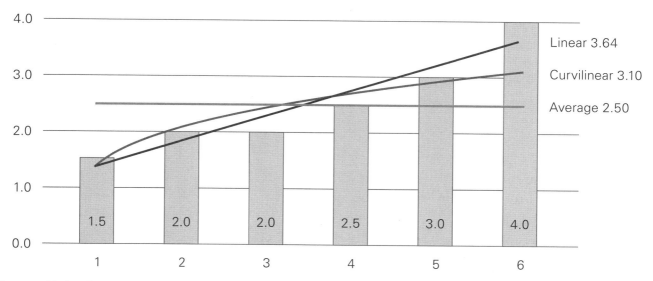

Figure 3.1: Three prediction lines.

In the introduction, I introduced the idea of one line cutting through a set of observed scores for a single student. In figure 3.1, notice that there are three lines cutting through the data. Each line represents a specific set of assumptions about the student's scores over time. The three lines represent the linear trend, the curvilinear trend, and the average. For each line, the final (the summative) predicted score is also reported. I consider each of these three prediction lines independently: (1) the linear trend line, (2) the curvilinear trend line, and (3) the trend line for the average. I then move on to reconciling the models.

The Linear Trend Line

The linear trend is represented by the straight line rising from the bottom left to the top right of the graph in figure 3.1. The basic assumption of this model is that student learning occurs in equal steps or increments. If the assessments are spaced equally apart, then the line representing the growth in true score will be a straight line gradually getting higher as depicted in figure 3.2. This model of learning is fairly ubiquitous in the research literature (Willett, 1985, 1988).

Note that each point where the linear trend line crosses the bar graph has a score that is different from the observed score represented by the bar graph. These are the predicted true scores from the linear trend model. The final predicted score of 3.64 can be considered the summative score. This is a very important aspect of the approach of mathematical models. Each model provides a predicted true score for each observed score. This is impossible in the traditional approach to reliability. With the method of mathematical models, one has a predicted true score for each observed score, for each student, for each mathematical model.

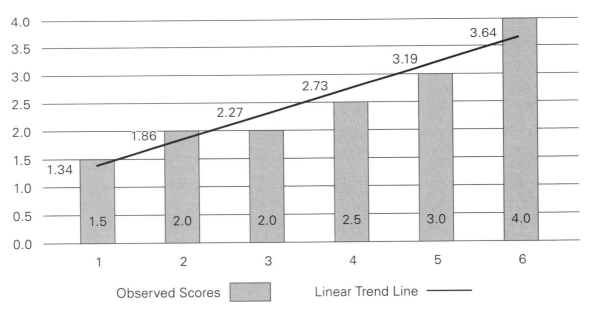

Figure 3.2: Linear predicted and observed scores.

The Curvilinear Trend Line

The curvilinear trend progresses from the lower left to the upper right, as does the linear trend. However, the curvilinear trend tends to flatten out as time goes on. This is depicted in figure 3.3.

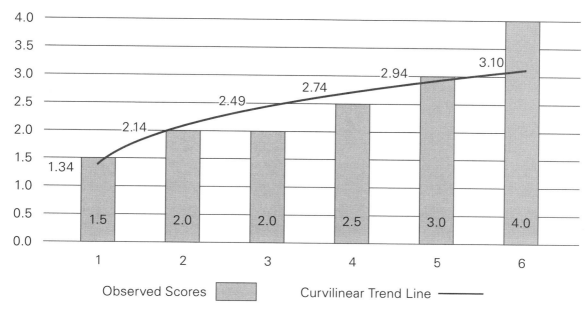

Figure 3.3: Curvilinear predicted and observed scores.

The assumption underlining this model is that learning begins with rather large increases, but those increases get smaller and smaller as the learner develops greater levels of expertise. This is demonstrated by comparing the predicted scores for the curvilinear model with the predicted scores of the linear model. Note that the curvilinear model predicts higher true scores for assessments 1, 2, 3, and 4 but not for assessments 5 and 6. The final predicted (summative) score for the curvilinear model is 3.10, whereas the final predicted score for the linear model is 3.64.

John R. Anderson (1995) notes that the curvilinear model seems to fit a variety of types of learning studied in cognitive psychology.

The Average Trend Line

The average is represented by the horizontal line in the graph. This model assumes that no learning has occurred from assessment to assessment. Rather, the difference in observed scores is simply due to random error in the individual assessments. This is depicted in figure 3.4 (page 68).

Notice that in figure 3.4, the predicted scores are always 2.50. This will necessarily be the case when the average is used to estimate the true scores from assessment to assessment.

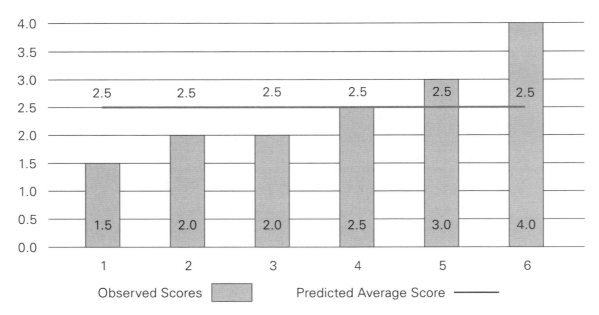

Figure 3.4: Average predicted and observed scores.

Model Reconciliation

The method of mathematical models generates three distinct sets of predicted true scores for each assessment for each student—each predicted score being based on a specific set of assumptions about learning. The final predicted score can be considered the summative score for each model. Of course, these three summative scores are different. If we used the linear model, we would estimate the summative score to be 3.64; if we used the curvilinear model, we would estimate it to be 3.10; and if we used the average, we would estimate it to be 2.50.

How does one decide which mathematical model to use for the summative score? Fortunately, there is a fairly straightforward approach to reconciling the different predicted scores. This approach involves identifying the model of best fit.

Model of Best Fit

The model of best fit is the one whose predicted scores are closest to the observed scores. To illustrate, see figure 3.5. Consider the third assessment, which had an observed score of 2.00. The predicted score using the linear trend was 2.27, which is 0.27 units away from the observed score. The predicted score using the curvilinear trend was 2.49, which is 0.49 units away from the observed score, and the predicted score using the average was 2.50, which is 0.50 units away from the observed score. Thus, for the third score in the set, the linear trend has the predicted score that is closest to the observed score. If one computes the differences between predicted and observed scores in the three models for each score, one can determine which model best fits the observed data.

Assessment		1	2	3	4	5	6	Total Difference	Average Difference
Observed Score		1.50	2.00	2.00	2.50	3.00	4.00		
Linear	**Predicted Linear Trend Score**	1.34	1.86	2.27	2.73	3.19	3.64		
	Difference From Observed Score	0.16	0.14	0.27	0.23	0.19	0.36	1.36	0.227
Curvilinear	**Predicted Curvilinear Trend Score**	1.34	2.14	2.49	2.74	2.94	3.10		
	Difference From Observed Score	0.16	0.14	0.49	0.24	0.06	0.90	1.99	0.332
Average	**Predicted Averaged Trend Score**	2.50	2.50	2.50	2.50	2.50	2.50		
	Difference From Observed Score	1.00	0.50	0.50	0.00	0.50	1.50	4.00	0.667

Note: The difference between the predicted score and the observed score is reported as an absolute value, which means that the difference does not include a negative or positive sign.

Figure 3.5: Best-fit calculator.

Figure 3.5 contains the observed scores and predicted scores for each model. It also includes the differences between each model's observed and predicted scores. Finally, it reports the total and average differences between the observed and predicted scores for each model. These totals and averages clearly indicate that the linear trend–predicted scores fit the observed data best.

When the line of best fit is identified, the most precise estimate of the student's true scores across the assessments is now available, and the best-fit model's final predicted true score can be considered the most precise estimate of the student's true summative score. In this case, the best estimate of the true summative score is 3.64.

Again, this is a critical point to remember about the method of mathematical models. It uses the observed scores to mathematically estimate true scores. The provided model estimates are based on different assumptions about the nature of growth for each student across a specific set of assessments on a particular topic. Once you identify the line of best fit, you can consider the predicted true scores from that model the official estimates of the true score on each assessment.

Using Technology

The calculations for the method of mathematical models are not designed for classroom teachers to do by hand. Clearly, technology is required to use these mathematical models. Technical notes 3.1, 3.2, and 3.3 (page 111) provide all necessary formulas and explanations to create a viable system using an Excel spreadsheet or similar software. Additionally, educators can consult empowerlearning.net for illustrations as to how the method of mathematical models can be displayed electronically to make identification of a precise summative score quite easy. Figure 3.6 depicts a basic input screen that you can create using the information in those technical notes.

	1	2	3	4	5	6	7	8	9	10	11	12	13	14	15	16	17	18	19	20
1	1.0				1.5						2.0			2.0			2.5			2.5
2	1.5										3.0				3.0			3.5		3.5
3	2.0		2.0								3.0									4.0
4	1.0		1.5								2.5					3.0		3.5		3.5
5	2.0					2.5					2.5			3.0			3.5			4.0

Figure 3.6: Basic input screen.

Figure 3.6 depicts the scores of five students entered into the spreadsheet over a twenty-day interval of time (not counting weekends). Note that each column represents a specific day beginning with the first assessment, and each row represents a specific student. All scores relate to one measurement topic only.

Figure 3.6 is an illustration only, designed to fit the constraints of a printed book. A spreadsheet designed to be used during a grading period should have enough columns for each day during the grading period and each student in a particular class.

On the first day of the grading period depicted in figure 3.6, the teacher administered a traditional test for a specific measurement topic and recorded students' scores. As noted, the first student received a score of 1.0, the second a score of 1.50, and so on. Each student received an initial score on the same day.

During the next nine days, students received scores, but not all students were assessed every day. Students 3 and 4 received scores on day 3, but no one else did. Student 1 was the only one to receive a score on day 5, and student 5 was the only one to receive a score on day 6. Over days 2 through 10, students were assessed individually using a differentiated approach as described in chapter 2. These individual assessments took the forms of probing discussions, observations, student-generated assessments, student self-assessments, and the like.

On day 11, the teacher gave an assessment to the entire class, and all students received a score. After that, the teacher differentiated assessments until the twentieth day, during which he or she administered another assessment to the entire class and assigned scores to each student.

This spreadsheet provides a great deal of information that needs to be summarized for the teacher. The three trend lines for each student as depicted in figures 3.2, 3.3, and 3.4 (pages 66, 67, and 68, respectively) can also be generated from this spreadsheet. In addition, a teacher can construct a best-fit report like that in figure 3.7.

Day of Assessment	1	5	11	14	20	Predicted Summative Score	Average Error
Observed Score	2.00	3.00	3.00	3.50	3.50		
Linear Trend Line							
Predicted True Score	2.179	2.733	2.963	3.516	3.608	3.608	
Error	0.179	0.267	0.037	0.016	0.108		0.121
Curvilinear Trend Line							
Predicted True Score	1.987	2.990	3.149	3.416	3.451	3.451	
Error	0.013	0.010	0.149	0.084	0.049		0.061
Trend Line for the Average							
Predicted True Score	3.00	3.00	3.00	3.00	3.00	3.00	
Error	1.00	0.00	0.00	0.50	0.50		0.400

Note: Error is reported as absolute values.

Figure 3.7: Best-fit report.

The report in figure 3.7 is for a specific hypothetical student. Reports like these are continually generated for each student.

The first row of figure 3.7 identifies the days on which observed scores were entered for the student. For this student, scores were entered on days 1, 5, 11, 14, and 20. The next row contains the observed scores. They were 2.00, 3.00, 3.00, 3.50, and 3.50.

The next two rows pertain to the linear model. The first of these rows contains the predicted true score using the linear trend line. The second row in this set reports differences in the predicted and observed scores. For example, the observed score for the first assessed day was 2.00. The predicted score for the linear trend was 2.179. The difference was 0.179; this is referred to as *error*. The second-to-last column contains the predicted summative score of 3.608. This will always be the same as the final score in the pattern of predicted scores. Finally, the last column contains the average error for the linear trend. This is 0.121. This is simply the average absolute difference between the observed score and predicted. The two rows for the curvilinear trend contain the same type of information as do the two rows for the average.

To identify the line of best fit, the teacher needs only examine the average error for the three models. In this case, the curvilinear trend has an average error of 0.061, which is much smaller than the average error from the linear trend (0.121) and the average error from the average (0.400). Therefore, the curvilinear trend contains the most precise estimate of the students' true scores across the assessments.

Now, we can round up or round down versus using the predicted scores. One convention that is becoming popular is to round up or down to the nearest half-point or quarter-point when reporting the summative scores. For example, consider the best-fit summative true score for the student in figure 3.7. This is 3.451. For purposes of a report card, some districts and schools use a rounding algorithm. In this case, whether the school or district uses a quarter-point or half-point system, the reported summative score would be 3.50. Interestingly, whether the curvilinear trend or the linear is used, the rounded score would also be 3.5. This indicates strong evidence that the estimated true score is fairly accurate.

Discussing the Implications for Formative and Summative Scores

The preceding discussion sheds light on a significant problem with some manifestations of formative and summative assessment. The distinction between formative and summative assessments became enormously popular when Paul Black and Dylan Wiliam (1998a, 1998b) published their findings of a comprehensive narrative review of literature on assessments. In that study, they caution about overgeneralizing their findings since the studies they reviewed were quite diverse:

> Individual quantitative studies which look at formative assessment as a whole do exist . . . although the number with adequate and comparable quantitative rigour would be of the order of 20 at most. However, whilst these are rigorous within their own frameworks and purposes, and whilst they show some coherence and reinforcement in relationship to the learning gains associated with classroom assessment initiatives, the underlying differences between the studies are such that any amalgamations of their results would have little meaning. (Black & Wiliam, 1998a, pp. 52-53)

Despite Black and Wiliam's (1998a) warnings, the notion that formative assessment in and of itself could dramatically increase student learning became quite popular, and many commercially prepared assessments became tagged as formative in nature even though the validity of these claims was questionable (see Popham, 2006). Soon, within the measurement community, researchers began to disagree as to the importance and utility of formative assessment (see Briggs, Ruiz-Primo, Furtak, Shepard, & Yin, 2012; Kingston & Nash, 2011).

In a later work, Wiliam (2016) explains many of the reasons for the confusion regarding formative assessment's nature and effects. One issue on which he focuses was the fundamental nature of formative assessment: "Perhaps the most important variable is the theory of action implied in the approach to formative assessment. Put simply, what exactly is the formative assessment meant to *form*?" (p. 113). The somewhat obvious answer to Wiliam's (2016) question from the perspective of this book is that they are meant to provide evidence that allows teachers to form estimates of students' true scores as precisely as possible with the given data. Unfortunately, some manifestations of formative and summative scores actually hinder the estimation of the most precise scores.

Some districts and schools view all formative assessments as practice for summative assessments. Students take these practice assessments, but the scores are not recorded. When students are ready to take the summative assessment, they record scores. If their observed score is above a certain cut score on the summative assessment, they are considered proficient. If they score below the cut score on the summative assessment, they engage in more instructional activities and practice assessments and then take another summative assessment when they appear ready.

The obvious problem with this approach is evident from the discussion about standard error of measurement. The score a student receives on any summative assessment contains error. Assume a student receives a score of 79 on a summative assessment, and assume that 80 is the cut score, so the student is not judged proficient. However, as we have seen, even if this assessment has a reliability of 0.85, the student's true score could be up to about six points higher or six points lower.

From the perspective of this book, formative scores should be tracked for individual students since they generate the data necessary to compute mathematical trends. Additionally, a summative assessment is not necessary to assign a summative score, especially since any single score will have a good deal of error operating around the observed score. In fact, I have recommended that the terms *formative assessments* and *summative assessments* be replaced by the terms *formative scores* and *summative scores* (Marzano, 2010).

Any time a teacher has information that provides concrete evidence that a particular student is at a particular level on a particular proficiency scale, the teacher should record a score for the student in question. This implies that a teacher is collecting and recording formative scores on students almost continually. In fact, in this system, a teacher might rely on traditional tests quite infrequently. Additionally, as described in the previous section, a teacher might not administer a formal summative assessment, instead opting to use the pattern of formative scores to assign a summative score.

Using Instructional Feedback

Many of the discussions of strategies that are labeled as formative assessments fall into what I have referred to as *instructional feedback*. In *Formative Assessment and Standards-Based Grading* (Marzano, 2010), I elaborate on this point. Briefly, though, any assessment information that is not recorded as a formative score is instructional feedback. For example, a teacher might administer a practice test to all students and immediately go over the answers as students score their own papers. While a score has been generated for each student, their scores are not recorded, even though the teacher and the students have a better understanding of their level of knowledge and skill regarding the topic. This is instructional feedback. As another illustration, a teacher uses voting technologies to obtain a sense of students' knowledge of score 2.0 content. However, the teacher does not record these scores. This is instructional feedback. Using this distinction between instructional feedback and formative scores can go a long way in alleviating the current confusion in the field regarding formative assessment.

Employing the Method of Mounting Evidence

As previously described, using the formulas in technical notes 3.1, 3.2, and 3.3 (page 111), educators can create software that allows teachers to use the method of mathematical models to evaluate the pattern of scores for each student. Ideally, a district or school should take the responsibility to create software that all teachers can use. If a teacher does not have access to the method of mathematical models, then he or she can employ the method of mounting evidence.

In this method, the teacher examines the pattern of scores a student has exhibited each time he or she enters a new score in a gradebook. When she feels confident, the teacher then makes an estimate of the student's true score. To illustrate, assume that for a particular measurement topic, a student has received the following two scores: 2.0 and 2.5. The teacher has just had a probing discussion with the student for which she has assigned an observed score of 3.0. The teacher feels confident that she has enough data to hypothesize a true score. Looking at the data, she concludes that at this point, the score of 3.0 probably is the best estimate of the true score. To test her hypothesis, the teacher asks two questions. First, if the student's true score is 3.0, how likely is it that he or she would exhibit this pattern? To answer this question, the teacher uses all available information about the student, including information from instructional feedback that was not recorded. If the teacher can confidently conclude that the answer to the question is very likely, then the teacher moves to the next question. If the student's true score is lower than 3.0, how likely is it that he or she would exhibit this pattern? If the teacher can confidently conclude that the answer to this question is very unlikely, then the teacher can confidently record a score of 3.0 as the best estimate of the student's true score at that point of time.

Assigning probability estimates to the answers to these two questions helps teachers quantify the level of certainty regarding their conclusions. Figure 3.8 depicts a scale for different levels of certainty.

Very Likely
Likely
Neutral
Unlikely
Very Unlikely

Figure 3.8: Levels of certainty.

It is important to note that a teacher can assign numerical probabilities to each level of certainty in figure 3.8. Technical note 3.4 (page 115) discusses this in depth. Here we simply consider answering the two questions from the perspective of this highly informal approach to levels of certainty. Again, the two questions follow.

1. If the student's true score is X, how likely is it that he or she would exhibit this pattern?

2. If the student's true score is lower than X, how likely is it that he or she would exhibit this pattern?

If the answer to the first question is *very likely* and the answer to the second question is *very unlikely*, then the teacher can record her estimate of the true score with confidence. As a matter of fact, under a certain set of assumptions that technical note 3.4 addresses in depth, the teacher can be about 90 percent sure that the student's true score is not lower than the estimated score. Even if the teacher can answer *very likely* for the first question and *unlikely* (as opposed to *very unlikely*) to the second question, the teacher can be about 75 percent sure that the estimate is accurate. A teacher should be able to answer the first question as *very likely* and the second as *very unlikely* or *unlikely* to confidently record a hypothesized true score. Although this approach is not as rigorous as the method of mathematical models, it actually has a relatively sound mathematical basis known as Bayesian probability (Bays, 1764; see technical note 3.4).

To see how this approach might manifest in the classroom, see figure 3.9.

	MT 1		MT 2		MT 3		MT 4		MT 5	
Chayla	1.5	4.0		4.0		4.0		4.0		4.0
	2.0	3.0		3.0		3.0		3.0		3.0
	2.5	2.0		2.0		2.0		2.0		2.0
		1.0		1.0		1.0		1.0		1.0
David	2.0	4.0		4.0		4.0		4.0		4.0
	2.5	3.0		3.0		3.0		3.0		3.0
	3.5	2.0		2.0		2.0		2.0		2.0
		1.0		1.0		1.0		1.0		1.0
Burke	3.0	4.0		4.0		4.0		4.0		4.0
	3.0	3.0		3.0		3.0		3.0		3.0
	3.5	2.0		2.0		2.0		2.0		2.0
		1.0		1.0		1.0		1.0		1.0

Figure 3.9: Method of mounting evidence.

continued ⇨

Eryn	2.5	4.0		4.0		4.0		4.0		4.0
	3.0	3.0		3.0		3.0		3.0		3.0
	3.0	2.0		2.0		2.0		2.0		2.0
	4.0	1.0		1.0		1.0		1.0		1.0
Alicia	3.0	4.0		4.0		4.0		4.0		4.0
	4.0	3.0		3.0		3.0		3.0		3.0
	3.5	2.0		2.0		2.0		2.0		2.0
		1.0		1.0		1.0		1.0		1.0

Note: MT stands for measurement topic.

This grade sheet in figure 3.9 has room for five measurement topics, MT 1 through MT 5. Each cell depicts scores for a specific student on a single topic, and a column at the right of each cell has four boxes labeled 4.0, 3.0, 2.0, and 1.0. This column is where the hypothesized true scores are recorded. Observed scores are entered to the left of the column with boxes.

Consider the first student, Chayla, and the first measurement topic. Chayla has three observed scores: 1.5, 2.0, and 2.5. Let's assume that up until the third observed score, the teacher did not believe he had enough information about Chayla to hypothesize a true score. However, once he recorded the third observed score, the teacher felt like there was enough information with which to hypothesize a true score. The teacher's first hypothesis was that the true score was 2.5. About this hypothesized true score, he asked the first question: "If Chayla's true score is 2.5, how likely is it that Chayla would exhibit this pattern?" The teacher answers this as *very likely*. The second question was, If Chayla's true score is lower than 2.5, how likely is it she would exhibit this pattern? After briefly thinking about the assessment evidence for Chayla and even his informal interactions with her, the teacher concludes that the answer to this question is *neutral*. However, this does not meet the threshold to confidently record the hypothesized true score. The teacher then drops his estimate back by a half point to 2.0 and answers *very likely* to the first question and *very unlikely* to the second question. Therefore, the teacher records a true score of 2.0 at this point in time. As the teacher continues to make decisions about Chayla's current estimated true score, he can be more and more sure that the estimate is precise. Technical note 3.4 (page 115) describes the variations in decision patterns for this approach in some depth.

Considering the Issue of Scales

One topic that sometimes comes up regarding the use of proficiency scales or even learning progressions as the basis of CAs is that they represent ordinal scales and are not accurate enough to be applied to students' status or growth on a particular topic. While this criticism is not as common as it was, it still occasionally arises, particularly when proficiency scales are used in place of the traditional one hundred–point scale. Therefore, the topic is worth a concise but substantive discussion. We'll discuss proficiency scales as inherently ordinal; proficiency scales that are internally consistent; and the strong statistics theory.

The issue of scales as they relate to education measurement began in 1946 with a publication by S. S. Stevens titled "On the Theory of Scales of Measurement." He later expanded on this first publication (Stevens, 1951, 1959, 1960). Fundamentally, Stevens (1951, 1959, 1960) made distinctions between four different types of measurement scales: (1) ratio, (2) interval, (3) ordinal, and (4) nominal. Their characteristics and the types of mathematical operations that are appropriate in each type are reported in table 3.2.

Table 3.2: Four Types of Scales

Scale	Acceptable Inferences	Allowable Mathematical and Statistical Operations
Ratio	Determination of equality of ratios	• Coefficient of variation such as the ratio of the standard deviation to the mean
Interval	Determination of equality of intervals and differences	• Mean • Standard deviation • Rank order correlation • Product moment correlation
Ordinal	Determination of greater or lesser	• Median • Percentiles
Nominal	Determination of equality	• Number of cases • Mode • Contingency correlation

As depicted in table 3.2, once one gets below the level of an interval scale, very few mathematical operations can be performed. For example, according to Stevens (1951, 1959, 1960), you cannot generate a mean or standard deviation with data from an ordinal scale.

The issue as Stevens articulated it was referred to as the *weak measurement theory* and became quite controversial (see Baker, Hardyck, & Petrinovich, 1966; Burke, 1953; Lubin, 1962; Senders, 1953). This theory is particularly problematic for classroom teachers and CAs since education measures are typically based on ordinal scales. This is because the intervals between numbers on the scale can be quite different. Edward L. Thorndike (1904) highlighted the problem of scale in education testing over one hundred years ago. He notes that given a test that is scored on a 0 to 100 scale:

> Suppose now that one boy in Latin is scored 60 and another 90. Does this mean, as it would in ordinary arithmetic, that the second boy has one and one half times as much ability or has done one and one half times

as well? It may be chance in some cases, but the fact that the best one and the worst one of thirty boys may be so marked by one teacher, and during the next half year in the same study be marked 70 and 90 by the next teacher, proves that it need not. The same difference in ability may, in fact, be denoted by the step from 60 to 90 by one teacher, by the step from 40 to 95 by another, by the step of from 75 to 92 by another and even by still another by the step from 90 to 96. Obviously school marks are quite arbitrary and their use at their face value as measures is entirely unjustifiable. A 90 boy may be four times or three times or six fifths as able as an 80 boy. (Thorndike, 1904, p. 7)

Thorndike (1904) further explains that the nature of academic content in K–12 education does not lend itself to equal units. This can be demonstrated by using even such a seemingly concrete subject as spelling. To illustrate, Thorndike (1904) analyzes the spelling tests of J. M. Rice administered in 1895 (see the introduction, page 2) and concludes that there exist no comparable units from spelling word to spelling word. Is the ability to correctly spell the word *certainly* correctly equal to the ability to spell the word *because*?

In effect, Thorndike (1904) was exposing the inherent weaknesses of the one hundred–point scale that has become so popular in K–12 education. Table 3.3 easily demonstrates the vagaries of the scales created through the one hundred–point or percentage system.

Table 3.3: Point Assignments of Student Scores

Item Number	Student Response	Point Assignment Scenario A	Student Points Earned	Point Assignment Scenario B	Student Points Earned	Point Assignment Scenario C	Student Points Earned
1	Completely correct	2	2	6	6	10	10
2	Completely correct	2	2	6	6	10	10
3	Completely correct	5	5	8	8	12	12
4	Half correct	10	5	10	5	14	7
5	Half correct	12	5	14	7	16	8
Total		31	19	44	32	62	47
Percent			61%		73%		76%

Table 3.3 presents three scenarios (A, B, and C) for a single assessment that includes five items. In all three cases, the student answers the first three items completely correctly and receives full points for each. However, the student is only half correct for items 4 and 5 and therefore receives only half of the

points associated with these items. While the student response pattern for the items stays the same in all scenarios, the points assigned to them are different.

In scenario A, the five items have been assigned the following points: two, two, five, ten, and twelve. Under this weighting scheme, the student receives a percentage score of 61. Scenario B has a different scheme for assigning points to items. Under this scheme, the student receives a percentage score of 73. Under scenario C, the student receives a percentage score of 76. Clearly, the different weighting of items dramatically changes the nature of the scale underlying this five-item test. In effect, assigning different points to items creates a different scale for each scenario.

The issue of equivocal scales in schools becomes even more acute when teachers average tests together. A student has a score of 87 on one test, a score of 50 on another, and a score of 77 on the third. The average of these is 71. This seems logical on the surface, but consider the makeup of the tests. The first test measured relatively easy content, the second test measured more complex content, and the third test measured very difficult content. This average score of 71 provides very little information that can be trusted in terms of its precision.

Proficiency Scales as Inherently Ordinal

Proficiency scales are particularly susceptible to the criticism of the weak measurement theory. They seem to be inherently ordinal because there is no guarantee that the competence levels from one level to another are equidistant. For example, do the knowledge and skill necessary for a student to move from a score value of 1.0 to 2.0 on a proficiency scale represent the same interval of improvement as the knowledge and skill necessary to move from a score value of 3.0 to 4.0? According to the measurement theory, the scores produced using the scale are unreliable. Virginia L. Senders (1953) demonstrates this problem using an illustration like that in figure 3.10.

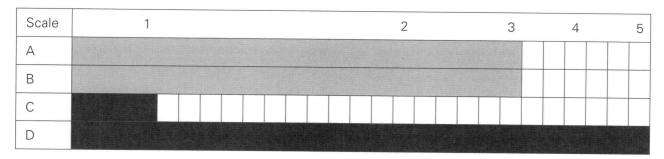

Source: Adapted from Senders, 1953.

Figure 3.10: Senders demonstration scale.

In figure 3.10, the first row represents a scale that is clearly an ordinal scale because the distances between the score values are so different. The difference between 0 and 1 is relatively small, but the difference between score values 1 and 2 is very large. The differences between score values 3 and 4 and 4 and 5 are also small but equal.

This would seem to present a problem with adding scores from this scale. To illustrate, consider the four measurements in the figure: A, B, C, and D. Item A received a score of 3, as did item B. If we added these together, the sum would be 6. Item C had a score of 1, and item D had a score of 5. If we added these together, the sum would also be 6, but it's obvious that the combined length of A and B is longer than the combined length of C and D. As Senders (1953) notes the "number assigned to the objects total 6 in both cases, but inspection will reveal that the additions of the objects will give a longer line" (pp. 423–424) in the first case than in the second.

For these reasons, some question the utility of proficiency scales to accurately measure students' status and growth. Interestingly, some educators reject the use of proficiency scales because they are ordinal and opt for the one hundred–point scale even though it is no less ordinal than proficiency scales.

If one accepts the weak measurement theory for CAs, then there is little the classroom teacher can do. They can't combine tests in any way whether they utilize proficiency scales or the one hundred–point scale. They can't combine scores to form overall grades. Overall grades can't be used to generate grade point averages (GPAs). GPAs can't identify valedictorians and so on. Fortunately, it is not necessary to take these drastic measures for at least two reasons: the internal consistency of proficiency scales and the strong statistics history.

Proficiency Scales That Are Internally Consistent

Proficiency scales as described in this book are immune to many of the issues of the weak measurement theory. This is because scores assigned to different students within a specific proficiency scale are comparable even if the intervals within the scale are not equal. To illustrate, consider figure 3.11, which depicts a proficiency scale that has unequal intervals.

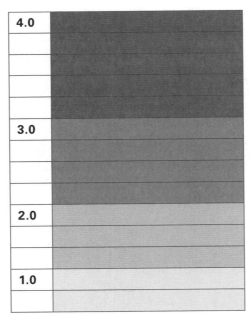

Figure 3.11: Proficiency scale with unequal intervals.

In the case of figure 3.11, the interval of knowledge gain is different at each level of the scale. The shortest amount of knowledge gain is between 0.0 and 1.0. The next largest interval of gain is between score 1.0 and 2.0 and so on. Clearly, the intervals between each score level are unequal. However, when students are assigned scores on the scale via the measurement process, they must demonstrate comparable knowledge gain from level to level simply because the content necessary to master at each level has been articulated—that is, the fact that each level of a proficiency scale explicitly describes what students should know and be able to do to move to the next level renders the progress within each level of the scale similar from student to student. To move from score 2.0 to 3.0 requires each student to demonstrate knowledge of the same content. To move from score 3.0 to 4.0 requires each student to demonstrate knowledge of the same content even though there is more of a content difference between score 3.0 and 4.0 than there is between score 2.0 and 3.0. While there will certainly be measurement error every time a score is assigned to a student, this error is not exacerbated by the scale itself.

This noted, the internal consistency within proficiency scales due to the measurement process does not address the issue of combining scores from different proficiency scales into an average—that is, it doesn't address what happens when a teacher averages scores across measurement topics to come up with an overall (omnibus) score or grade. I consider this issue in chapter 5 (page 93). However, this issue is addressed well by the strong statistics theory.

The Strong Statistics Theory

Another reason that teachers should not be overly concerned with the ordinal nature of proficiency scales is that the weak measurement theory has been countered by the strong statistics theory. Specifically, proponents of the strong statistics theory proposed and demonstrated that scores for ordinal scales can and should be manipulated through operations like addition, subtraction, multiplication, and division. For example, one study found that statistical analyses of data from ordinal, interval, and ratio scales basically produce the same results (Baker et al., 1966). The authors note that "the present findings indicate that strong statistics . . . are more than adequate to cope with weak measurements—and, with some minor reservations, probabilities estimated . . . are little affected by the kind of measurement scale used" (Baker et al., 1966, p. 308). Similar findings have also been reported (see Carifio & Perla, 2007; Knapp, 1990).

In simple terms, the strong statistics theory posits that when teachers perform statistical operations on scores from ordinal scales, the errors associated with the scales themselves tend to cancel each other out. In effect, then, classroom teachers can perform their usual practices of computing averages using scores from proficiency scales without undue concern.

Summary

This chapter began with an examination of the classical test theory's paradigm for reliability and its historical development. The classical test theory paradigm for reliability gradually evolved to the ratio of the true score variance to the observed score variance. This allows the reliability of a test to be estimated from a single administration of the test. While useful for large-scale assessments, this perspective offers classroom teachers few options. A new and more appropriate paradigm for CAs is to estimate true scores across a set of parallel assessments. Three mathematical models are offered to this end: (1) the linear trend, (2) the curvilinear trend, and (3) the average. The model of best fit can be identified by examining the errors for each model that are operationally defined as the aggregate differences between observed scores and predicted scores. The best-fit predicted scores are the most precise estimate of true scores available across a set of parallel assessments. Another method of estimating true scores across a set of assessments relies on a teacher making a series of estimates about a student's true score at a given point in time. As the teacher makes more estimates, he or she can be more sure that the current estimate is precise. This is referred to as the method of mounting evidence. Finally, the criticism that proficiency scales are ordinal and, therefore, should not be manipulated mathematically by operations like addition, subtraction, multiplication, and division is addressed. This criticism is invalid for at least two reasons. First, proficiency scales are internally consistent, allowing teachers to mathematically manipulate students' scores within a specific proficiency scale. Second, the strong statistics theory has demonstrated that the errors associated with ordinal scales tend to cancel out each other. This allows teachers to manipulate scores for students across proficiency scales.

Now I'll discuss measuring growth for groups of students.

chapter 4

Measuring Growth for Groups of Students

In chapter 3, I addressed the precision (reliability) of the scores for individual students on a specific topic. This is the primary role of CAs—to generate scores for individual students on specific measurement topics that are as close to each student's true scores as possible. The method of mathematical models provides teachers with tools for doing this. In this scenario, reliability or precision is defined as determining the model that best fits the observed score data. One might say that this type of reliability is designed to answer the question, On this particular topic, what is the most precise score that you can assign to each student on each assessment over time? While not as rigorous a process mathematically, the method of mounting evidence also provides reasonably precise estimates of students' true scores, particularly at the end of a series (and particularly for their summative scores).

Estimating the true scores on assessments for individual students on a specific topic is not the only concern of a classroom teacher, though. Rather, comparative student growth is also of interest. A teacher might want to analyze how much one student has grown in a particular topic in comparison to other students in the class or compared to other students in other classes. This might also be of interest to school administrators or district administrators. As we will see in chapter 5, depicting student growth on report cards provides useful information to students, teachers, and parents. Therefore, measuring the growth of groups of students in a reliable manner is beneficial to virtually all constituents in a district, school, or classroom.

When group growth is the focus, then, reliability must be addressed differently from the procedures described in chapter 3. This means that educators must think in terms of two types of reliability for CAs: one that deals with the scores for individual students on sets of parallel assessments (called *precision*) and one that deals with the comparative growth of students (called *reliability*).

This second type of reliability is designed to answer the question, What is the most precise comparable measure of students' growth? To answer this question, the students within a class are treated as a group, and each student's growth is considered a score. This puts us back into the classical paradigm for reliability where the scores of individual students on a particular test are analyzed as a set. Since we are now using the paradigm for classical test theory, it is more appropriate to use the term *reliability* as opposed to the term *precision*, which applies to individual students. The first step in the process of computing this type of reliability is to determine the measure of student growth that will be used to compare groups of students. I'll also cover reconciling the three reliabilities, as well as using technology.

Measuring Growth

As would be the case with determining the traditional reliability of a single test, to determine the reliability of a set of growth scores, we need "observed scores" for each student. In this case, though, the scores represent each student's growth over time. You can use three types of growth scores: (1) the linear growth score, (2) the curvilinear growth score, and (3) the difference score.

Linear Growth Score

As its name implies, the linear growth score is computed right from the linear trend line described in chapter 3 (page 59). The technical name for the linear growth score is the *slope* of the trend line. In more general terms, it is referred to as the *linear growth parameter* (Collins & Sayer, 2001; Willett, 1985, 1988). For the purposes of this book, I will use the term *linear growth score* since it is probably more descriptive and understandable in the context of CAs. However, when more useful, I also use the term *slope*. To illustrate the linear growth score, consider figure 4.1.

Figure 4.1 depicts two trend lines, each with different linear growth scores (slopes). Each linear trend line comes from a different student: student A and student B. The more learning that has occurred for a student, the steeper the slope and the larger the growth score. In figure 4.1, it's obvious that student B has the steeper slope and demonstrates the most learning. This is evident in his or her linear growth scores. Student A has a linear growth score of 0.56; student B has a linear growth score of 0.93.

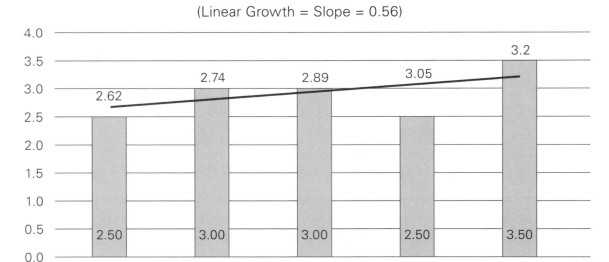

Student A

(Linear Growth = Slope = 0.56)

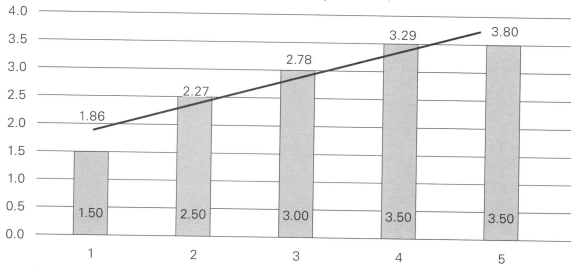

Figure 4.1: Linear growth.

Linear growth scores (slopes) range from 0.0 to +1.0 and down to −1.0. The larger the linear growth score, the more learning. A student with a linear growth score of 0.80 would be said to have learned more than a student with a linear growth score of 0.40. If a linear growth score were negative (has a minus sign in front of it), it means that student learning has regressed and the line would go from the top left to the bottom right. This should rarely occur for a student unless there is a great deal of measurement error across assessments.

The formula for the reliability of a set of slopes follows.

Reliability of slopes for a set of students = variance of the true slopes / variance of the observed slopes

Again, this is the classical test theory formula described in chapter 2 with one major change: the scores for which variances for true and observed scores are computed are growth scores (slopes) as opposed to raw scores on a test. To illustrate, consider table 4.1 (page 86).

In table 4.1, each of ten students has a linear growth score computed from a pattern of scores in a particular measurement topic as described in chapter 3. Using the formulas in technical note 4.1 (page 118)—and a certain set of assumptions about score precision for individual students—the reliability of these ten scores is 0.76 and can be interpreted in the same way as a traditional reliability coefficient. Specifically, it provides an estimate of how much or how little these growth scores can be expected to change if the entire process that generated these scores were repeated without students recalling their previous performance.

Table 4.1: Linear Growth Scores

Student	Growth Score
Student 1	0.85
Student 2	0.91
Student 3	0.81
Student 4	0.72
Student 5	0.85
Student 6	0.72
Student 7	0.94
Student 8	0.57
Student 9	0.82
Student 10	0.78
Reliability = 0.76	

The Curvilinear Growth Score

As described in chapter 3, the curvilinear trend model produces a curved line of predicted true scores like those depicted in figure 4.2.

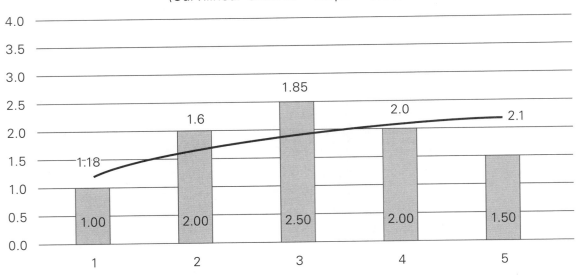

Student C
(Curvilinear Growth = Slope = 0.66)

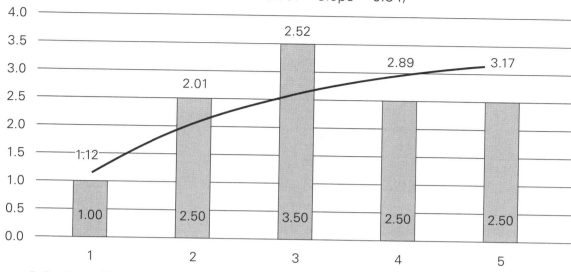

Figure 4.2: Curvilinear growth.

Again, there are two lines representing the curvilinear growth for two different students (C and D). Student D seems to be the one with the most growth. Unfortunately, curvilinear trends do not have a single slope as do linear trends, so the growth score is not as obvious. Fortunately, there are well-accepted ways to compute a curvilinear growth score that is directly comparable to the linear growth score. The formula for this is in technical note 3.2 (page 112). Using that formula, student C obtains a curvilinear growth score of 0.66, but student D receives a higher growth score of 0.84, thus verifying what can be inferred from visual inspection of the two graphs.

After graduating the curvilinear growth scores, teachers can compute the reliability using the formulas in technical note 4.2 (page 120). Consider the curvilinear growth score for the ten students in table 4.2.

Table 4.2: Curvilinear Growth Scores

Student	Growth Score
Student 1	0.78
Student 2	0.81
Student 3	0.84
Student 4	0.62
Student 5	0.82
Student 6	0.71
Student 7	0.78

continued ⇨

Student	Growth Score
Student 8	0.92
Student 9	0.84
Student 10	0.77
Reliability = 0.84	

The reliability of these ten slopes is 0.84, which is higher than the reliability of the linear growth score for the same ten students. Comparing linear and curvilinear growth scores indicates that, thus far, the curvilinear trend is the more reliable.

The Difference Score

The third type of growth score that can be computed when considering the reliability of growth across students is the difference score (also referred to as the gain score). As its name implies, the difference score is simply the difference between a student's first observed score and final score during a given grading period. Consider figure 4.3.

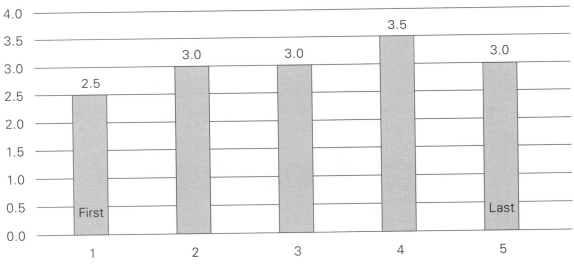

Student E
(Gain = Last Minus First = 0.50)

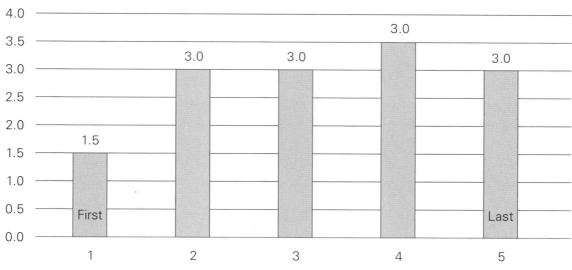

Figure 4.3: Gain score.

In figure 4.3, student E started with an observed score of 2.5 and ended with an observed score of 3.0 for a gain score of 0.50. Student F started with an observed score of 1.5 and ended with an observed score of 3.0 for a gain of 1.5.

Obviously, the gain for each student is quite easy to compute, resulting in a set of difference scores. Consider table 4.3.

Table 4.3: Gain Score

Student	Growth Score
Student 1	1.0
Student 2	2.5
Student 3	2.0
Student 4	0.5
Student 5	2.0
Student 6	0.5
Student 7	2.0
Student 8	3.0
Student 9	2.0
Student 10	1.0
Reliability = 0.42	

A very different formula must be used to compute the reliability of difference scores. This is described in technical note 4.3 (page 121). Briefly, though, it requires estimates of the reliability of the first assessment and the last assessment for each student. As described in technical note 4.3, standard formulas for computing these single test reliabilities can be used or reliabilities can be estimated.

Using the formulas in technical note 4.3, we compute the reliability of the differences score to be 0.42. This is much lower than the reliabilities computed for the linear slopes or the curvilinear slopes, which is often the case. One reason is that difference scores only use two data points for each student (first and last scores), whereas trend scores use all formative scores for students. This is evident from figure 4.3. Note that student E began with a score of 2.5 and ended with a score of 3.0 for a gain of 0.5. However, this does not count the fourth score of 3.5, which showed a gain of 1.0 from the initial score. Difference scores include only the first and last scores in a series, whereas linear and curvilinear growth scores use all scores within a set to compute a growth score.

Reconciling the Three Reliabilities

We now have three types of growth scores and three estimates of reliability: (1) reliability of the linear slope, (2) reliability of the curvilinear slope, and (3) reliability of the difference scores. When comparing the growth of student groups, it is important to use the growth measure that demonstrates the highest level of reliability. Consider table 4.4, which depicts the three types of growth reliabilities across five classes.

Table 4.4: Three Types of Reliabilities Across Five Classes

	Linear Reliability	Curvilinear Reliability	Difference Score Reliability
Class 1	0.76	0.84	0.42
Class 2	0.85	0.86	0.52
Class 3	0.79	0.77	0.47
Class 4	0.82	0.92	0.65
Class 5	0.85	0.93	0.72
Average	0.81	0.88	0.56

Recall that the question about the data from these classes is, What is the most precise comparable measure of growth of students? The five classes depicted in table 4.4 would have used the same proficiency scale for the same unit of instruction. Of the three types of reliability, curvilinear reliability had the highest average across the five classes. The average reliability for linear growth was 0.81, the average reliability for curvilinear growth was 0.88, and the average reliability for the difference score was 0.56. This means that for purposes of comparison, the growth of each class would be the curvilinear growth score.

Again, it is important to emphasize the fact that this is a different perspective from that presented in chapter 3. This perspective certainly does not contradict the perspective in chapter 3. It simply looks at different information—the growth of the students in a class considered as a group versus the precision of scores for individual students. In chapter 3 we were concerned with finding the most precise true score estimate for each student using three mathematical models: (1) the linear trend, (2) the curvilinear trend, and (3) the average. While the most precise true score estimates might come from the linear model for one student, they might come from the curvilinear model for another student and from the average for still another student. In this chapter, we are considering the average growth for the entire class, but we have three ways to measure growth: (1) the linear growth score, (2) the curvilinear growth score, and (3) the difference score. To compare the average growth across classes, we must select one type of growth measure to apply to all classes. The one with the highest average reliability is the growth score that should be used for comparative purposes. In chapter 5 (page 93), I show how this approach can be used with student learning objectives.

Using Technology to Help Teachers

As before, districts and schools should create technology-based software that computes reliabilities for the three types of growth scores. Educators can design such programs using technical notes 4.1, 4.2, and 4.3 (page 118) and the resource provided by Haystead and Marzano (2017). Table 4.5 depicts a type of report that can help teachers easily discern the best growth scores to use. Consider table 4.5, which illustrates.

Table 4.5: Reliability of Growth Score for Five Students

Model	Reliability
Linear Growth	0.634
Curvilinear Growth	0.771
Difference Scores	0.000

The reliabilities in table 4.5 are computed from the scores for five students reported in figure 3.6 in chapter 3 (page 70). The reliability of the linear growth scores across the five students is 0.634; the reliability of the curvilinear growth score is 0.771; and the reliability of the difference scores is 0.000. This is a relatively common pattern when there are very few students in a class. For the linear and curvilinear reliabilities, this is understandable from the perspective of the formula for the reliability coefficient. Recall that this formula is as follows.

> Reliability of linear or curvilinear growth score = true variance of growth score / observed variance of growth scores

If the growth scores for a set of students are too similar, then reliability will automatically be low. This is a basic principle of the classical test theory model of reliability. To illustrate, assume that five students receive precisely the same linear or curvilinear growth scores across a set of scores. In this case, the variance of observed scores would be zero, producing a reliability coefficient of zero. Significant differences in observed scores is one of the assumptions underlying the use of the traditional reliability coefficient. If observed scores are too similar, the reliability coefficient will automatically be low.

The same holds true for the reliability of difference scores, although the explanation is a little more complex. (For a discussion, see technical note 4.3 on page 121.) When only five sets of scores are available, there are not enough data to ensure a requisite level of variability.

To address the issue of low variability, I recommend that at least ten students be in a data set before reliability can be effectively computed. Usually with this number of students, you can compute reasonable estimates of growth reliability. Consider table 4.6.

Table 4.6: Reliabilities of Growth Scores for Ten Students

Model	Reliability
Linear Growth	0.938
Curvilinear Growth	0.932
Difference Score	0.754

Table 4.6 reports the growth reliabilities for the same set of students used in table 4.5 except for the fact that scores for five more students have been added. In this case, the linear growth reliability has increased to 0.938, the curvilinear growth reliability has increased to 0.932, and the difference score reliability has increased to 0.754.

Summary

This chapter examines the reliability of growth measures for a group of students. This type of reliability becomes important when teachers or administrators wish to compare the growth of one class versus another or rank the growth of several classes. In such cases, a growth score is assigned to each student using three types of scores: the linear growth score, the curvilinear growth score, and the difference score. To determine which of these types of growth scores should be used to compare growth between classes, the reliability of each type is computed. The type of growth score with the highest reliability is the one that is used for comparative purposes. In all cases, reliability estimates will be deflated when there are too few students in a class.

Next, I discuss how to transform the system using the new paradigms.

chapter 5

Transforming the System Using the New Classroom Assessment Paradigms

The new paradigms for CAs have the potential of transforming the K–12 system far beyond measurement in the classroom. Taken to their logical endpoints, these paradigms can influence many aspects of schooling that might seem unrelated on the surface. Here we consider two areas of transformation: (1) report cards and (2) teacher evaluations.

Transforming Report Cards

Ultimately, most teachers must translate students' summative scores for measurement topics addressed during a grading period into an overall or omnibus grade. This can be done using the new paradigms for CA, but the report card will contain more information than traditional report cards. Consider figure 5.1.

Name	Lori Fedorowicz
Address	1230 Grape Street
City	Anytown, CO 80000
Grade Level	5

Figure 5.1: Report card.

continued ⇨

Language Arts	2.56	B−
Mathematics	3.18	A−
Science	2.56	B−
Social Studies	2.94	B+
Art	2.75	B

Generating Conclusions	2.70	B
Navigating Digital Sources	3.50	A
Staying Focused	3.00	A−
Seeking Accuracy	3.00	A−

		0.5	1.0	1.5	2.0	2.5	3.0	3.5	4.0

English Language Arts

		0.5	1.0	1.5	2.0	2.5	3.0	3.5	4.0
Decoding	2.5								
Analyzing Text Organization and Structure	1.5								
Analyzing Ideas and Themes	2.0								
Analyzing Claims	3.5								
Analyzing Narratives	2.5								
Comparing Texts	1.0								
Analyzing Words	2.5								
Generating Text Organization and Structure	3.0								
Generating Sentence Structure	3.0								
Generating Claims	3.0								
Using Citations	2.5								
Generating Narratives	2.5								
Generating Point of View and Purpose	3.0								
Writing for a Specific Audience	3.0								

Using Specific Words and Parts of Speech	3.0	
Punctuation, Capitalization, and Spelling	2.0	
Revision and Editing	3.0	
Average for English Language Arts	2.56	
Cognitive Skills (English Language Arts)		
Generating Conclusions	2.5	
Navigating Digital Sources	3.5	
Metacognitive Skills (English Language Arts)		
Staying Focused	3.0	
Seeking Accuracy	3.0	
Mathematics		
Decimals	3.0	
Fractions	3.0	
Area	3.0	
Volume	2.5	
Multiplication	3.5	
Division	3.5	
Comparison Symbols	4.0	
Exponents	3.0	

continued ⇨

Ordered Pairs and Coordinate Systems	3.0
Addition and Subtraction	4.0
Perimeter	4.0
Data Representation	3.0
Central Tendency in Data Sets	3.0
Numerical Patterns	3.0
Probability	3.0
Symmetry	3.0
Two-Dimensional Figures	4.0
Basic Functions	2.5
Factors and Multiples	2.5
Measurement	3.0
Average for Mathematics	3.18
Cognitive Skills (Mathematics)	
Generating Conclusions	3.0
Navigating Digital Sources	3.5
Metacognitive Skills (Mathematics)	
Staying Focused	3.5
Seeking Accuracy	3.5
Science	
Matter and its Interactions	2.5

Motion and Stability: Forces and Interactions	3.0	
Energy	3.0	
From Molecules to Organisms: Structures and Processes	2.5	
Ecosystems: Interactions, Energy, and Dynamics	2.0	
Earth's Place in the Universe	2.0	
Earth's Systems	2.0	
Earth and Human Activity	3.0	
Engineering Design	3.0	
Average for Science	2.56	
Cognitive Skills (Science)		
Generating Conclusions	2.5	
Navigating Digital Sources	3.5	
Metacognitive Skills (Science)		
Staying Focused	2.5	
Seeking Accuracy	2.5	
Social Studies		
History: Analyze and Interpret Historical Sources	3.5	
History: Historical Eras, Individuals, Groups, Ideas, and Themes in Regions of the Western Hemisphere	3.5	
Geography: Use Geographic Tools	3.0	

continued ⇨

Geography: Human and Physical Systems	3.0
Economics: Different Economic Systems	2.5
Economics: Personal Financial Literacy	3.0
Civics: Connection of the United States to Other Nations	2.5
Civics: Multiple Systems of Government	2.5
Average for Social Studies	2.94
Cognitive Skills (Social Studies)	
Generating Conclusions	3.0
Navigating Digital Sources	3.5
Metacognitive Skills (Social Studies)	
Staying Focused	3.0
Seeking Accuracy	3.0
Art	
Perceptual Skills and Visual Arts Vocabulary	3.0
Art Elements and Principles of Design	3.0
Skills, Processes, Materials, and Tools	2.5
Communication and Expression Through Original Works of Art	2.5

Average for Art	2.75										
Cognitive Skills (Art)											
Generating Conclusions	2.5										
Navigating Digital Sources	3.5										
Metacognitive Skills (Art)											
Staying Focused	3.0										
Seeking Accuracy	3.0										

The bar graphs in figure 5.1 represent a student's proficiency scale scores on specific measurement topics. The dark part of each bar graph indicates a student's first score at the beginning of the year. The light part of each bar graph represents the student's score on a proficiency scale at the end of the grading period. As discussed previously, students' final or summative scores should be computed using mathematical models that best fit the data. If this is not possible, summative scores can be compiled using the method of mounting evidence. For reporting purposes, these scores are rounded up or down to the nearest half-point or quarter-point score.

In figure 5.1, the overall score for a subject area in the report card is computed by averaging the final scores on measurement scale topics. To illustrate, consider English language arts. The measurement topics addressed in this subject area are Analyzing Text Organization and Structure; Analyzing Ideas and Themes; Analyzing Claims; Analyzing Narratives; Comparing Texts; Analyzing Words; Generating Text Organization and Structure; Generating Sentence Structure; Generating Claims; Using Citations; Generating Narratives; Generating Point of View and Purpose; Writing for a Specific Audience; Using Specific Words and Parts of Speech, Punctuation, Capitalization, and Spelling; and Revision and Editing. The summative scores for these measurement topics were averaged to obtain the aggregate score of 2.56. This is not the only way to aggregate scores. Here, we consider the strengths and weaknesses of some of the more common approaches: weighted and unweighted averages; the median and the mode; the conjunctive approach; a supplemental measurement topic; and the practice of allowing students to increase their scores.

Weighted and Unweighted Averages

The most common approach to combining summative scores is to compute an unweighted average. To illustrate, consider an individual student with the following seven summative scores at the end of a grading period: 1.5, 2.5, 2.5, 3.5, 3.0, 3.0, and 3.5. The average of these scores is 2.79. This average can be converted to an overall letter grade or percentage grade using the conversion scale in table 5.1 (pages 100–101).

Table 5.1: Conversion Scale

Scale Score	Percentage	Grade	Scale Score	Percentage	Grade	Scale Score	Percentage	Grade	Scale Score	Percentage	Grade
4.00	100	A	2.30 to 2.34	76	C	1.30 to 1.31	50	F	0.73 to 0.75	25	F
3.90 to 3.99	99	A	2.25 to 2.29	75	C	1.28 to 1.29	49	F	0.70 to 0.72	24	F
3.80 to 3.89	98	A	2.20 to 2.24	74	C	1.26 to 1.27	48	F	0.67 to 0.69	23	F
3.70 to 3.79	97	A	2.15 to 2.19	73	C	1.24 to 1.25	47	F	0.64 to 0.66	22	F
3.60 to 3.69	96	A	2.10 to 2.14	72	C	1.22 to 1.23	46	F	0.61 to 0.63	21	F
3.50 to 3.59	95	A	2.05 to 2.09	71	C	1.20 to 1.21	45	F	0.58 to 0.60	20	F
3.40 to 3.49	94	A	2.00 to 2.04	70	C	1.18 to 1.19	44	F	0.55 to 0.57	19	F
3.30 to 3.39	93	A	1.95 to 1.99	69	D	1.16 to 1.17	43	F	0.52 to 0.54	18	F
3.20 to 3.29	92	A	1.90 to 1.94	68	D	1.14 to 1.15	42	F	0.49 to 0.51	17	F
3.10 to 3.19	91	A	1.85 to 1.89	67	D	1.12 to 1.13	41	F	0.46 to 0.48	16	F
3.00 to 3.09	90	A	1.80 to 1.84	66	D	1.10 to 1.11	40	F	0.43 to 0.45	15	F
2.95 to 2.99	89	B	1.75 to 1.79	65	D	1.08 to 1.09	39	F	0.40 to 0.42	14	F

Grade	Score	Range	Grade	Score	Range	Grade	Score	Range	Grade	Score	Range
B	88	2.90 to 2.94	D	64	1.70 to 1.74	F	38	1.06 to 1.07	F	13	0.37 to 0.39
B	87	2.85 to 2.89	D	63	1.65 to 1.69	F	37	1.04 to 1.05	F	12	0.34 to 0.36
B	86	2.80 to 2.84	D	62	1.60 to 1.64	F	36	1.02 to 1.03	F	11	0.31 to 0.33
B	85	2.75 to 2.79	D	61	1.55 to 1.59	F	35	1.00 to 1.01	F	10	0.28 to 0.30
B	84	2.70 to 2.74	D	60	1.50 to 1.54	F	34	0.98 to 0.99	F	9	0.25 to 0.27
B	83	2.65 to 2.69	F	59	1.48 to 1.49	F	33	0.96 to 0.97	F	8	0.22 to 0.24
B	82	2.60 to 2.64	F	58	1.46 to 1.47	F	32	0.94 to 0.95	F	7	0.19 to 0.21
B	81	2.55 to 2.59	F	57	1.44 to 1.45	F	31	0.91 to 0.93	F	6	0.16 to 0.18
B	80	2.50 to 2.54	F	56	1.42 to 1.43	F	30	0.88 to 0.90	F	5	0.13 to 0.15
C	79	2.45 to 2.49	F	55	1.40 to 1.41	F	29	0.85 to 0.87	F	4	0.10 to 0.12
C	78	2.40 to 2.44	F	54	1.38 to 1.39	F	28	0.82 to 0.84	F	3	0.07 to 0.09
C	77	2.35 to 2.39	F	53	1.36 to 1.37	F	27	0.79 to 0.81	F	2	0.04 to 0.06
			F	52	1.34 to 1.35	F	26	0.76 to 0.78	F	1	0.01 to 0.03
			F	51	1.32 to 1.33				F	0	0.00

As mentioned in chapter 4 (page 83), a potential problem with using an average is that each proficiency scale is basically ordinal in nature. As we have seen, this is not an issue when assigning scores within the context of a specific scale. However, those who take the weak measurement perspective would argue that growth of 1.0 unit on one scale is not necessarily the same as growth of 1.0 unit on another scale. In contrast, those who take the strong statistic perspective would assert that even though interval sizes differ from scale to scale, performing operations like computing an average is legitimate given that the inconsistency between scales tends to cancel out. I take this latter position.

A version of the unweighted approach is the weighted approach. Here, one or more of the topics receives more weight than other topics. For example, consider the seven topic scores previously listed. If the first and second scores were to receive twice the weight as all other scores, the average for the seven would change from 2.79 to 2.61.

The Median and the Mode

Some schools have adopted the practice of using the median or the mode as a summary score for a set of topics. The *median* is the middle score in a set of scores. For example, assume that a student received the following summative scores at the end of a grading period for eight different measurement topics: 2.0, 2.0, 2.5, 2.5, 2.5, 3.0, 3.5, 4.0. The middle score here is 2.5, which is different from the unweighted average of 2.75.

Use of the median has some positive aspects. If one adheres to the weak measurement theory, it does help alleviate the issue of ordinal scales not having equal intervals. However, if one takes the strong statistics perspective, then the unweighted or weighted average is probably better since each provides interpretations that are more common to students, teachers, and parents. If one accepts the strong statistical theory, then the average would be preferable.

The *mode* is the most common score in a set. For the set of eight summative scores previously listed, the mode is 2.5, which is the same as the median. I typically do not recommend the mode because it can produce an overall score that is highly misleading. To illustrate, consider the following set of summative scores: 1.0, 1.0, 1.5, 2.0, 2.5, 3.0, 3.5, 4.0. The mode in this set is 1.0. The median is 2.25, and the average is 2.313. Clearly, the mode does not provide a very useful representation of the student's overall score across the measurement topics. Another problem with the mode is that it can be equivocal. To illustrate, consider the following distribution of scores: 1.0, 2.0, 3.0, 3.0, 4.0, 1.0. This distribution is *bimodal*, which means it has two modes: 1.0 and 3.0. Again, this does not provide a useful depiction of the student's overall achievement.

The Conjunctive Approach

Of all the approaches to combining summative scores for students presented in this chapter, the conjunctive approach makes the most sense. Most approaches are compensatory approaches (Kifer, 1994; Marzano, 2006, 2010). A compensatory approach is one in which high scores compensate for low scores. Using the weighted and unweighted averages are compensatory approaches because a high score of 4.0

will compensate for a low score of 1.0. In a less direct manner, the median might be considered a compensatory approach.

The conjunctive approach is quite different (Plake, Hambleton, & Jaeger, 1995). As it relates to grading, I initially introduced it in the book *Classroom Assessment and Grading That Work* (Marzano, 2006) and expanded on it in the book *Formative Assessment and Standards-Based Grading* (Marzano, 2010). Marzano et al. (2017) illustrate the conjunctive approach for the measurement topics in mathematics as depicted in table 5.2. Each measurement topic has a proficiency scale, and nine measurement topics were introduced in the first trimester. These are listed in the first column. However, for three of the topics, instruction did not progress beyond the score 2.0 content. In addition, students only just started learning about score 3.0 content in two of the topics. The level of exposure to each topic is addressed in the second column.

Given that for three of the topics students did not receive instruction beyond score 2.0 content and for two of the topics they received only partial instruction on the score 3.0 content, the teacher might establish criteria for a grade of A as depicted in the last column of table 5.2.

Table 5.2: Scoring Criteria for a Grade of A for First Trimester

Measurement Topic	Exposure to Content	Criteria
Decimals	Complete	3.0 or above
Fractions	Just started score 3.0 content	2.5 or above
Area	Score 2.0 content only	2.0 or above
Volume	Score 2.0 content only	2.0 or above
Multiplication	Complete	3.0 or above
Division	Complete	3.0 or above
Ordered Pairs and Coordinate Systems	Score 2.0 content only	2.0 or above
Addition and Subtraction	Complete	3.0 or above
Perimeter	Just started score 3.0 content	2.5 or above

Notice that in this scheme, a student can receive a grade of A with a score of 2.0 on the measurement topics of area, volume, and ordered pairs and coordinate systems, and a score of 2.5 on fractions and perimeter.

For a grade of B, the teacher might use the minimum scores depicted in table 5.3 (page 104).

Table 5.3: Scoring Criteria for a Grade of B for First Trimester

Measurement Topic	Exposure to Content	Criteria
Decimals	Complete	2.5 or above
Fractions	Just started score 3.0 content	2.0 or above
Area	Score 2.0 content only	1.5 or above
Volume	Score 2.0 content only	1.5 or above
Multiplication	Complete	2.5 or above
Division	Complete	2.5 or above
Ordered Pairs and Coordinate Systems	Score 2.0 content only	1.5 or above
Addition and Subtraction	Complete	2.5 or above
Perimeter	Just started score 3.0 content	2.0 or above

The teacher would use a similar approach to set minimum scores for grades of C, D, and F. As this example illustrates, the conjunctive approach can be useful in a standards-referenced system when students have not been exposed to all the score 2.0 and score 3.0 content for some measurement topics during a grading period.

A Supplemental Measurement Topic

One problem that frequently comes up when designing a standards-referenced system of reporting is that teachers want to address content that is not contained in the proficiency scales for the grade level and subject area. This is probably a natural tendency on the part of teachers since the content in the fifteen to twenty-five measurement topics their school or district has designed might exclude some content they consider important. To allow for the inclusion of this important but excluded content, some schools have included a supplemental measurement topic in every reporting cycle. Previously, I have referred to such a topic as a *residual measurement topic* (see Marzano & Haystead, 2008). Here I use the term *supplemental measurement topic* because it seems to resonate better with parents, students, teachers, and administrators.

If a school or district opts to include a supplemental measurement topic, it should be clear about what it can include. Generally, the school or district should control the content in the supplemental category. Content in the supplemental category should be important enough for the school or district to have time devoted to it for direct instruction. As described by Heflebower et al. (2014), teachers can identify this content via a process of unpacking the knowledge and skills in standards into three categories: (1) content for which proficiency will be developed and measured, (2) content taught directly but not a part of a proficiency scale, and (3) content that might be briefly mentioned or addressed if time allows. Content in this second category might be included in the supplement measurement topic.

Of course, a measurement problem that immediately arises is that the assessments regarding the content in the supplemental category are not unidimensional. Therefore, teachers cannot design parallel assessments, and they cannot track student growth. This issue notwithstanding, teachers can construct a generic proficiency scale for this multidimensional content. Consider figure 5.2.

Score 4.0	Students analyze content in ways that have not been directly addressed in class. Analyses require students to form new conclusions and defend their answers.
Score 3.5	In addition to score 3.0 performance, partial success at score 4.0 content
Score 3.0	Students identify the critical components of concepts, generalizations, and principles, and can articulate how those parts interact. If content is process oriented, students can execute the process without error and with fluency.
Score 2.5	No major errors regarding score 2.0 content and partial success at score 3.0 content
Score 2.0	Students recognize or recall important vocabulary, and students recognize or recall important details. If content is process oriented, students can perform simple versions of the process.
Score 1.5	Partial success at score 2.0 content and major errors or omissions regarding score 3.0 content
Score 1.0	With help, partial success at score 2.0 and score 3.0 content
Score 0.5	With help, partial success at score 2.0 content but not at score 3.0 content
Score 0.0	Even with help, no success

Figure 5.2: Proficiency scale for multidimensional supplemental content.

Most content that falls into the supplemental category is easily expressed by teachers in terms of the descriptions for score 2.0, 3.0, and 4.0 in figure 5.2. Consequently, when a teacher designs an assessment for a supplemental topic, he or she describes the content for the topic at levels 2.0, 3.0, and 4.0 as outlined in the generic scale. However, since the supplemental category includes multiple topics, the best way to summarize the scores in the supplemental measurement topic is to simply compute their average.

The Practice of Allowing Students to Increase Their Scores

One powerful convention in grading that is available with the use of measurement topics is that students can increase their scores on topics covered previously. This fits into the research and theory on self-regulated learning. Specifically, Andrade (2013) explains that self-regulated learning engages students in four elements: (1) setting goals for their learning, (2) monitoring their progress toward the goal, (3) receiving and interpreting feedback, and (4) making adjustments based on feedback.

The report card in figure 5.1 provides a perfect infrastructure to implement this process if students can increase their scores on measurement topics from previous grading periods. Each new grading period, new measurement topics would be added to the report card and the overall grade would be based on the new measurement topics and the old. Additionally, teachers would provide students with opportunities to demonstrate their increase in status on previously scored measurement topics.

This dynamic allows students to implement the four steps of self-regulation. They set goals for the upcoming grading period relative to the new topics, and they set goals for raising scores on previous topics. Then they monitor their progress on the goals by examining feedback and making adjustments as necessary.

As mentioned in chapter 2 (page 39), the goals students set for themselves should be challenging but attainable. Referencing the work of Hattie (2009), Andrade (2013) explains that these goals should require students to do their best as opposed to simply meet some minimum standard. Indeed, goals students set should inspire them to strive for the highest scores they can reasonably achieve.

Transforming Teacher Evaluations

In July 2009, President Barack Obama and Secretary of Education Arne Duncan announced the Race to the Top (RTT) initiative with an overall budget of about $4.35 billion. The program offered states significant funding if they were willing to develop and implement more rigorous and comprehensive systems to evaluate teachers and principals. As stated in the U.S. Department of Education's (2010) *A Blueprint for Reform*:

> We will elevate the teaching profession to focus on recognizing, encouraging, and rewarding excellence. We are calling on states and districts to develop and implement systems of teacher and principal evaluation and support, and to identify effective and highly effective teachers and principals on the basis of student growth and other factors. (p. 4)

Clearly, President Obama and Secretary Duncan designed RTT to create an education system that more accurately differentiates between effective and ineffective teachers. Responding to this call, many (if not most) teacher evaluation systems included student growth. This emphasis is explicit in the RTT legislation and the literature surrounding that legislation. To be judged as effective, teachers must demonstrate that students have grown academically. The scores used to compute growth are commonly referred to as VAMs (value-added measures). Typically, state tests in reading and mathematics are used to compute VAMs.

On the surface, there is an intuitive logic to using VAMs: determine how much students have increased their scores on a common test after controlling for students' prior achievement and you have a good measure of how much value in learning has been added by the students' teacher. Unfortunately, this intuitive logic hasn't held up under close scrutiny. Marzano and Toth (2013) summarize three criticisms from the research literature.

1. **VAMs are test dependent:** Depending on the test that is used to compute students' growth scores, teachers receive different rankings.

2. **VAMs are formula dependent:** Depending on the mathematical formula that is used to compute students' growth scores, teachers receive different rankings.

3. **VAMs don't account for many important factors in students' learning:** Simply controlling for students' prior knowledge and demographic characteristics doesn't sort out other important factors in their growth like motivation, sense of efficacy, and support from home.

One of the biggest problems with VAMs as currently conceptualized is that most teachers do not teach grade levels or subject areas for which there are state tests. Specifically, Cynthia Prince and colleagues (2009) estimate that the traditional methods of computing VAMs that depend on state tests exclude 69 percent of teachers. To rectify this problem, districts have attempted to devise ways to measure student growth that can utilize locally designed assessments.

One of the most common approaches districts take is to use student learning objectives. As Brian Gill, Julie Bruch, and Kevin Booker (2013) describe, student learning objectives are clear-cut and quantifiable learning targets that measure increases in students' proficiency over time. Lisa Lachlan-Haché, Ellen Cushing, and Lauren Bivona (2012) describe a variety of approaches to creating student learning objectives. I have proposed an approach that utilizes the measurement process and proficiency scales as described in this book (see Marzano, 2006; Marzano, Basileo, & Toth, 2015).

Briefly, the approach is based on first designing common proficiency scales for teachers who teach the same subject area and grade level. The scales should address the content in a single unit of instruction that might range from two weeks to four weeks. A common pretest and posttest would be designed using the common scale. Teachers would administer the common pretest and posttest and score them with other teachers so that no teacher is the only one scoring the tests for his or her students. Between the common pretest and posttest, individual teachers design and administer their own assessments using a variety of forms (see chapter 2, page 39). Thus, at the end of the unit, all students will have taken the same pretest and posttest but will have been measured using intervening assessments that were designed by their teachers.

As described in chapter 4, with a common pretest and posttest in place and varied types and numbers of assessments in between, growth can be measured in three ways: the linear growth score, the curvilinear growth score, and the difference score. Educators would compute these scores and their reliabilities for each class in the set. Educators would then compare these reliabilities across classes to determine the type of growth that will be the basis for teacher comparisons. To illustrate, consider table 5.4.

Table 5.4: Teacher Comparisons

Teacher	Average Difference Score	Reliability of Difference Scores	Average Linear Growth	Reliability of Linear Growth	Average Curvilinear Growth	Reliability of Curvilinear Growth
1	1.53	0.25	0.81	0.84	0.92	0.81
2	2.01	0.43	0.91	0.92	0.87	0.91
3	1.77	0.58	0.88	0.87	0.90	0.84
4	1.03	0.71	0.84	0.84	0.83	0.84

continued ⇨

| 5 | 1.01 | 0.26 | 0.86 | 0.72 | 0.75 | 0.75 |
| Average | | 0.446 | | 0.838 | | 0.830 |

Table 5.4 provides a great deal of useful data for five teachers. Using the reliability column, it can be determined which of the three measures of growth is the most reliable indicator of student learning. In this case, the linear slopes have the highest reliabilities as their average demonstrates.

The slopes for each teacher can now be compared using the most reliable growth measure. In general, slopes of 0.50 or greater are considered strong (see Cohen, 1988). In this case, all teachers had average linear slopes much greater than this criterion, indicating effective growth in each classroom.

Perhaps more important than comparing teachers on the average growth of their students is how teachers set goals regarding the following.

- The average growth score in their class
- The lowest growth score in their class
- The reliability of growth scores in their class
- The percentage of different types of students who exhibit specific gain scores or slopes or both

To illustrate, a particular teacher might set a personal goal to have an average growth score (linear or curvilinear) of 0.80 or higher. Additionally, the teacher sets a goal that no student will have a growth score lower than 0.50. The teacher might also set a goal that at least one type of growth reliability will be higher than 0.75. Finally, the teacher sets a goal that specific students who have little academic support at home will have a gain score of at least 1.5 scale points.

Summary

This chapter has described two transformations that can and should occur in schools and districts based on the new paradigms for CAs. First, report cards can still report overall or omnibus grades and scores, but in addition, they should report students' status and growth on specific measurement topics. Additionally, teachers can provide students opportunities throughout the year to increase their status on any and all measurement topics addressed in a year. Second, teacher evaluation can be greatly aided by providing reliable and valid VAMs that utilize data from CAs focused on content directly taught by teachers and comparable from teacher to teacher.

To wrap up, using the concepts described in chapters 1 through 5 and the formulas in the appendix, teachers, schools, and districts can create tools that will render CAs equally (if not more) reliable and valid than the interim and end-of-year assessments that currently dominate K–12 education.

Technical Notes

Making Classroom Assessments Reliable and Valid is intended to raise the status of CAs in classrooms, schools, and districts. To do so requires the articulation of psychometric paradigms for validity and reliability different from those employed in the classical test theory. The new paradigm for validity includes CAs designed from highly focused proficiency scales that allow for the construction of parallel assessments scored using the measurement process.

Measurement, by definition, involves translating information for CAs into scores on proficiency scales. The new paradigm for reliability involves analyzing scores from parallel assessments for individual students. Mathematical analyses can provide estimates of each student's true score on each assessment. These types of analyses require programming using standard spreadsheet software. If such software and programming are not available, teachers can estimate the true score at the conclusion of a set of parallel assessments by examining mounting evidence. Finally, teachers can compare the growth of groups of students by identifying a common way of measuring growth across groups of students on a specific topic.

The technical notes in this appendix provide the formulas necessary for educators at the district, school, or classroom level to calculate the true score estimates and reliabilities described in previous chapters. I recommend that individuals knowledgeable about programming within a district or school create software that can be used by all teachers within the system.

- **Technical note I.1:** Confidence intervals
- **Technical note 3.1:** Linear trend line
- **Technical note 3.2:** Curvilinear trend line
- **Technical note 3.3:** Trend line for the average
- **Technical note 3.4:** The method of mounting evidence
- **Technical note 4.1:** Reliability of linear growth scores
- **Technical note 4.2:** Reliability of curvilinear growth scores
- **Technical note 4.3:** Reliability of difference scores

Technical Note I.1: Confidence Intervals

One can compute confidence intervals using the standard error of measurement (SEM), which is directly related to the reliability of an assessment. The formula for computing the SEM for an assessment is:

$$SEM = sd\sqrt{1 - Rel}$$

Where

sd = standard deviation

Rel = reliability

Based on this formula, SEM is a function of two variables: (1) the standard deviation for a set of test scores on a particular assessment, and (2) the reliability for the assessment. The higher the reliability, the lower the SEM. The smaller the standard deviation, the lower the SEM. To illustrate, consider the following table, table A.1.

Table A.1: The Relationship Among SEM, Reliability, and Standard Deviation

SEM	Reliability	Standard Deviation
3.87	0.85	10
7.75	0.85	20
5.92	0.65	10
3.87	0.85	10

In this table, I depict four scenarios—one scenario in each row. In the first two rows, the reliability stays the same (for example, 0.85), but the standard deviation changes. In the first row, the standard deviation is 10, and in the second row the standard deviation is 20. This change has a rather large effect on the SEM—when the standard deviation is 10, the SEM is 3.87; when the standard deviation is 20, the SEM is 7.75.

In the third and fourth rows, the standard deviation is held constant (for example, 10), but the reliability changes from 0.65 to 0.85. When the reliability is 0.65, the SEM is 5.92. When the reliability is 0.85, the SEM is 3.87.

To achieve a small SEM, then, an assessment should have a small standard deviation and a high reliability.

Once one determines an SEM, one can compute a confidence interval around any observed score. The theory underlying the concept of a confidence interval is as follows: any observed score on a test is a sample of a range of scores a student would receive on that same test if the student took the test repeatedly without remembering previous administrations and without changing in terms of his or her knowledge of the content on the test. Theoretically, one could conduct these reassessments an infinite number of times, forming a distribution of alternate scores around the observed score. A final set of assumptions is that this distribution of alternate scores would be normally distributed with the observed score as the mean of that distribution. The SEM, then, is the standard deviation of the distribution of possible scores around the observed score. This allows us to compute a confidence interval.

A very common practice in assessment design is to report the 95 percent confidence interval. To do so, one determines the scores in the normal distribution surrounding the observed score in which 95 percent of the hypothetical scores would fall. If we consult a table for the normal distribution, we find that 95 percent of the scores in a normal distribution fall between −1.96 standard deviations below the mean and +1.96 standard deviations above the mean. Since, we know that the observed score is the mean of that hypothetical distribution, we can compute the 95 percent confidence interval.

Assume that the observed score for a student is 75 on an assessment, and the standard error is 7.75. If we multiply 7.75 × 1.96, we obtain 15.19. Therefore, 1.96 standard deviations (that is, SEMs) below the observed score is 59.81, and 1.96 standard deviations (that is, SEMs) above the observed score is 90.19. Thus, the 95 percent confidence interval around a score of 75 for this particular assessment is 59.81 to 90.19.

Technical Note 3.1: Linear Trend Line

The basic equation for the linear trend line is:

$\hat{y} = mx + b + e$

Elements important to the evaluation of the equation include:

$\hat{y}$ = predicted true score

y = observed score

m = unstandardized slope

β = standardized slope

x = observed day of assessment

b = constant

e = error associated with the observed score

N = number of assessments

See figure A.1 (page 112).

Compute:	
Step 1: Unstandardized slope (*m*) from ordinary least squares (OLS) regression	$m = \dfrac{\sum xy - \dfrac{\sum x \sum y}{N}}{\sum x^2 - \dfrac{(\sum x)^2}{N}}$
Step 2: Constant (*b*) from OLS regression	$b = \dfrac{\sum y - m(\sum x)}{N}$
Step 3: Standardized slope (*β*) from OLS regression, also referred to as linear growth score	$\beta = \dfrac{\sum xy - N\bar{x}\bar{y}}{\sqrt{\sum x^2 - N\bar{x}^2}\ \sqrt{\sum y^2 - N\bar{y}^2}}$
Step 4: Predicted true score (*ŷ*)	$\hat{y} = mx + b$
Step 5: Residual score, also referred to as error (*e*)	$e = \hat{y} - y$
Step 6: Average error	$\bar{e} = \dfrac{\sum |\hat{y} - y|}{N}$
Report: *y*, *x*, *ŷ*, *β*, *e*, *ē*	

Figure A.1: Computing the linear trend line.

One computes the linear trend for an individual student across a set of scores on parallel assessments within a specific measurement topic. Any time a teacher enters a new score and its associated date of assessment, the linear trend line updates for that student. As described in previous chapters, the model for an individual student's score on a particular topic at a particular time is:

$$y_i = x_i(t_i) + e_i$$

Where y_i is the observed score at time i, x_i is the day of the assessment at time i, t_i is the true score at time i, and e_i is the error associated with the observed score at time i. The standardized slope β is considered the growth score for the data set.

Technical Note 3.2: Curvilinear Trend Line

The basic equation for the curvilinear trend line is:

$$\hat{y}_{LN} = m_{LN}x_{LN} + b_{LN} + e_{LN}$$

Elements important to the evaluation of the equation include:

$\hat{y}_{LN}$ = predicted true score in natural log form

$AL(\hat{y}_{LN})$ = antilog of the predicted true score in natural log form

y = observed score

m_{LN} = unstandardized slope when x and y are in natural log form

β_{LN} = standardized slope when x and y are in natural log form

x_{LN} = observed day of assessment in natural log form

x = observed day of assessment

b_{LN} = constant when x and y are in natural log form

e_{ALLN} = error associated with the observed score when x and y are in natural log form but $\hat{y}_{LN}$ has been translated back to the original metric

$\bar{e}_{ALLN}$ = average error associated with the observed score when x and y are in natural log form but $\hat{y}_{LN}$ has been translated back to the original metric

N = number of assessments

See figure A.2.

Compute:	
Step 1: Unstandardized slope (m_{LN}) when x and y are in natural log form	$m_{LN} = \dfrac{\sum x_{LN} y_{LN} - \dfrac{\sum x_{LN} \sum y_{LN}}{N}}{\sum x_{LN}^2 - \dfrac{(\sum x_{LN})^2}{N}}$
Step 2: Constant (b_{LN}) when x and y are in natural log form	$b_{LN} = \dfrac{\sum y_{LN} - m_{LN}(\sum x_{LN})}{N}$
Step 3: Standardized slope (β_{LN}) when x and y are in natural log form, also referred to as curvilinear growth score	$\beta_{LN} = \dfrac{\sum x_{LN} y_{LN} - N\bar{x}_{LN}\bar{y}_{LN}}{\sqrt{\sum x_{LN}^2 - N\bar{x}_{LN}^2}\ \sqrt{\sum y_{LN}^2 - N\bar{y}_{LN}^2}}$
Step 4: Predicted true score ($\hat{y}_{LN}$) when x and y are in natural log form	$\hat{y}_{LN} = m_{LN}x_{LN} + b_{LN}$
Step 5: Predicted true score when x and y are in natural log form but $\hat{y}_{LN}$ has been translated back to the original metric	$AL(\hat{y}_{LN}) = Antilog(\hat{y}_{LN})$
Step 6: Residual score when $\hat{y}_{LN}$ has been translated back to the original metric, also referred to as error (e_{ALLN})	$e_{ALLN} = AL(\hat{y}_{LN}) - y$
Step 7: Average error when $\hat{y}_{LN}$ has been translated back to the original metric	$\bar{e}_{ALLN} = \dfrac{\sum |AL(\hat{y}_{LN}) - y|}{N}$
Report: y, x, $AL(\hat{y}_{LN})$, β_{LN}, e_{ALLN}, $\bar{e}_{ALLN}$	

Figure A.2: Computing the curvilinear trend line.

One can compute a curvilinear trend using a variety of models that include a power function, an exponential function, and a quadratic function. While all of these are viable, they are not easy to compare with the linear trend in terms of a single growth parameter. Specifically, the linear trend employs the following equation.

$$\hat{y} = mx + b + e$$

This equation has a single growth parameter, m. In contrast, the power function employs the following equation.

$$\hat{y} = ax^b + e$$

In this equation, there are two growth parameters, a and b. A resolution to this issue is to transform both x and y variables into their natural logs and perform a simple OLS regression. This allows educators to analyze variables with a curvilinear relationship using a linear model. Hence, the basic equation for the curvilinear trend is now comparable to that for the linear save for the fact that variables are in natural log form.

$$\hat{y}_{LN} = m_{LN}x_{LN} + b_{LN} + e_{LN}$$

The growth parameter, m_{LN}, for the curvilinear model is now comparable to the growth parameter for the linear model. For reporting purposes, one must transform predicted scores and residuals into their original metrics (see steps 5, 6, and 7).

Technical Note 3.3: Trend Line for the Average

The basic equation for the trend line for the average is:

$$\hat{y} = \frac{\Sigma y}{N} + e$$

Elements important to the evaluation of the equation include:

$\hat{y}$ = predicted true score for each assessment

N = number of assessments

y = observed score

e = error associated with the observed score

See figure A.3.

Compute:	
Step 1: Predicted true score ($\hat{y}$)	$\hat{y} = \dfrac{\Sigma y}{N}$
Step 2: Residual score, also referred to as error (e)	$e = \hat{y} - y$
Step 3: Average error	$\bar{e} = \dfrac{\Sigma \lvert \hat{y} - y \rvert}{N}$
Report: $\hat{y}$, e, $\bar{e}$	

Figure A.3: Computing the trend line for the average.

The trend for the average is the simplest model that can predict the true score, because it does not assume that the true score for a student changes across parallel assessments. Consequently, the model predicts the same true score for all parallel assessments. This true score is the center of the distribution.

Technical Note 3.4: The Method of Mounting Evidence

The basic equation for the method of mounting evidence is:

$$p(A|B) = \frac{p(B|A)p(A)}{p(B|A)p(A) + p(B|\bar{A})p(\bar{A})}$$

Elements important to the evaluation of the equation include:

$p(A|B)$ = probability of event A given event B

$p(A)$ = probability of event A

$p(B|A)$ = probability of event B given event A

$p(\bar{A})$ = probability of event A not occurring, referred to as NOT A

$p(B|\bar{A})$ = probability of event B given NOT A

This equation is foundational to Bayesian probability, named for Thomas Bayes, an English clergyman who did early work in probability and decision theory. It can be used to determine how certain or uncertain one can be about specific combinations of events. William L. Hays (1973) offers the following practical illustration. In the middle of the night, a man gets out of bed to take a sleeping pill. He goes to the medicine cabinet, grabs one of the three bottles on the shelf, and takes a pill without reading the label on the bottle. He returns to his bed and starts feeling sick to his stomach. He suddenly remembers that two of the three bottles in his medicine cabinet contain sleeping pills but the other contains poison. He goes to the Internet and finds that 80 percent of the general population exhibit the symptoms he is having when they take the poison, and 5 percent exhibit the symptoms when they take a sleeping pill. Using the basic equation, one can compute the probability that the man has taken the poison.

If B represents the symptoms the man is having and A represents the event of taking the poison, then:

$p(B|A) = 0.80$

$p(B|\bar{A}) = 0.05$

If each bottle had an equal probability of being selected in the dark, then:

$p(A) = 0.33$

$p(\bar{A}) = 0.67$

Substituting these quantities in the basic equation gives:

$$p(A|B) = \frac{(0.80)(0.33)}{(0.80)(0.33) + (0.05)(0.67)} = 0.89$$

Therefore, one can conclude that there is a 0.89 probability that the man has taken the poison.

We can apply this approach to the method of mounting evidence by redefining the variables. Where $(B|A)$ stood for the probability of experiencing the symptoms (B) under the condition that the man had taken the poison (A), $(B|A)$ now stands for the probability of a student exhibiting the pattern of observed scores and behaviors (B) under the condition that the student's true score is the one the teacher is thinking of assigning (A). As explained in chapter 3, within the method of mounting evidence, the teacher periodically examines the assessment and instructional feedback evidence for students and records a current true score estimate. For example, when using the method of mounting evidence for a specific student, the teacher examines the student's previous and current scores along with her unrecorded behavior. This is (B). Based on this pattern, the teacher concludes that the student should be assigned a specific hypothesized true score on the proficiency scale. This is (A).

The teacher's ultimate goal is to determine how likely it is that the student would have the hypothesized true score from the proficiency scale (A), given the observed pattern of behavior (B). This is $(A|B)$, which represents the level of confidence that the teacher can place in the hypothesized true score.

To be able to compute $(A|B)$, the teacher must start with an estimate of $(B|A)$. The first question in the section in chapter 3 on the method of mounting evidence prompts the teacher to provide such an estimate: "If the student's true score is _____, how likely is it that he or she would have exhibited this pattern of scores and behaviors?" I provided five possible answers in chapter 4.

1. Very likely

2. Likely

3. Neutral

4. Unlikely

5. Very unlikely

To actually compute a Bayesian probability estimate, one has to assign numeric probabilities to the five proposed answers.

1. Very likely = 0.90

2. Likely = 0.70

3. Neutral = 0.50

4. Unlikely = 0.30

5. Very unlikely = 0.10

One also must assign a numeric probability to $(B|\bar{A})$. This stands for the probability of the student exhibiting the observed pattern of scores and behaviors (B) under the condition that the hypothesized true score on the proficiency scale is incorrect $(\bar{A})$. This estimate works best given the purposes of the method of mounting evidence, if we define $(\bar{A})$ to mean that the student's true score is something lower than the hypothesized true score the teacher wishes to assign. The second question in chapter 4 prompts this response: "If the student's true score is lower than _____, how likely is it that he or she would exhibit the observed pattern of scores and behaviors?" It is important that this question be answered independently of the first question. Again, the teacher assigns one of the five possible probability estimates.

1. Very likely = 0.90

2. Likely = 0.70

3. Neutral = 0.50

4. Unlikely = 0.30

5. Very unlikely = 0.10

To illustrate the interplay of the two questions that comprise the method of mounting evidence, assume that a teacher examines the pattern of observed scores and behaviors for a specific student and hypothesizes a true score of 3.0. The teacher asks the first question: "If the student's true score is 3.0, how likely is it that he or she would have exhibited this pattern?" The teacher concludes that it is very likely the student would exhibit the observed pattern if his or her true score were 3.0. This translates into a probability of 0.90 for $(B|A)$. The teacher then asks the second question: "If the student's true score is lower than 3.0, how likely is it that she would have exhibited this pattern of scores and behaviors?" The teacher concludes that it is unlikely. This translates into probability of 0.30 for $(B|\bar{A})$. The teacher doesn't assign a probability of very unlikely (0.10) because she can imagine situations in which a student could have that specific observed pattern of scores and behaviors but not know all the requisite 3.0 content. This might be the case in which the previous assessments for the student didn't adequately cover all the important content articulated at the score 3.0 level in the proficiency scale. The teacher concludes that it is unlikely (0.30) that the student's true score is lower than 3.0, but she can't say that it is very unlikely (0.10). We now have:

$(B|A) = 0.90$

$(B|\bar{A}) = 0.30$

To fully evaluate the equation, we still need estimates for (A) and $(\bar{A})$. (A) stands for the probability that the student could randomly receive a score of 3.0, and $(\bar{A})$ stands for the probability that the student could randomly receive a score lower than 3.0. This would occur if none of the student scores or behaviors the teacher was examining were reliable or valid measures of the content in the proficiency scale. Since we are considering only two possibilities (a true score of 3.0 [(A)], or a true score lower than 3.0 [$(\bar{A})$]), we can reasonably assign the probability of 0.50 to (A) and the probability of 0.50 to $(\bar{A})$. We now have the quantities necessary to evaluate the following equation.

$$p(A|B) = \frac{p(B|A)p(A)}{p(B|A)p(A) + p(B|\bar{A})p(\bar{A})}$$

$$p(A|B) = \frac{(0.90)(0.50)}{(0.90)(0.50) + (0.30)(0.50)} = 0.75$$

We can say that the probability of the hypothesized true score being accurate is 0.75. If the teacher had concluded that the probability of the student exhibiting the observed pattern if the true score were lower than 3.0 was very unlikely (0.10) as opposed to unlikely (0.30), then the probability of the hypothesized true score being accurate would have been 0.90. Either of these probabilities provides the teacher with fairly high confidence that the hypothesized true score is accurate.

It is important to note that the conclusion that the probability of a hypothesized true score is 0.75 or 0.90 is very different from the conclusion we can draw from confidence intervals from a single assessment. Recall that when a single assessment is given to students, the only recourse a teacher has when considering the precision of an individual student's score is to compute a confidence score around the observed score. In table I.2, we saw that even when an assessment has a reliability of 0.85, the confidence interval around an individual score had a range of about twelve points using a one hundred–point scale. Thus, if an individual student had an observed score of 75 on the test, the teacher would be 95 percent sure that the true score falls anywhere between 69 and 81. Where confidence intervals use a single assessment and focus on a range of possibilities, the method of mounting evidence uses all scores for a student and focuses on the level of certainly regarding a hypothesized true score based on all previous evidence. In summary, using the preceding Bayesian equation, the method of mounting evidence allows a teacher to say how likely it is that a student's true score is not lower than the one hypothesized by the teacher. If a teacher can answer the first question in the method of mounting evidence as highly likely and the second question as very unlikely or unlikely, then the teacher can be confident that the hypothesized true score is not an overestimate of the student's actual true score.

Technical Note 4.1: Reliability of Linear Growth Scores

The basic equation for reliability of linear growth scores is:

$$\rho_{\hat{\theta}} = \frac{\hat{\sigma}_{\theta}^2}{\sigma_{\hat{\theta}}^2}$$

Elements important to the evaluation of the equation include:

θ = growth parameter for an individual p

$\rho_{\hat{\theta}}$ = estimated reliability of the linear growth parameter

$\hat{\sigma}_{\theta}^2$ = estimated variance of the true linear growth parameter

$\sigma_{\hat{\theta}}^2$ = estimated variance of the observed growth parameter

MSE_p = mean squared error for an individual p

y = observed score for an individual p

$\hat{y}$ = predicted score for an individual p

$\hat{\sigma}_e^2$ = estimated measurement error variance

SST_p = variance of assessment time for an individual p

x_i = day on which specific assessment was administered

M_{SST} = estimated variance of observation times

m = unstandardized slope for an individual p

N_p = number of individuals in the set (class)

See figure A.4.

Compute:	
Step 1: Mean squared error for OLS regression for each individual p	$MSE_p = \dfrac{\Sigma(\hat{y} - y)^2}{N_p - 2}$
Step 2: Estimated measurement error variance—average of MSE_p from OLS regression for each individual p	$\hat{\sigma}_e^2 = \dfrac{\Sigma MSE_p}{N_p}$
Step 3: Variance of assessment times for each individual p	$SST_p = \Sigma(x_i - \bar{x})^2$
Step 4: Estimated variance of assessment times—average of SST_p for each individual p	$M_{SST} = \dfrac{\Sigma SST_p}{N_p}$
Step 5: Estimated observed growth parameter variance	$\sigma_\theta^2 = \dfrac{\Sigma(m - \bar{m})^2}{N_p - 1}$
Step 6: Estimated true growth parameter variance	$\hat{\sigma}_\theta^2 = \sigma_\theta^2 - \dfrac{\hat{\sigma}_e^2}{M_{SST}}$
Step 7: Estimated reliability of growth parameter	$\rho_\theta = \dfrac{\hat{\sigma}_\theta^2}{\sigma_\theta^2}$
Report: ρ_θ	

Figure A.4: Computing the reliability of linear growth scores.

As indicated by the basic equation, the reliability of the linear growth scores (for example, slopes or growth parameters) follows the traditional classical test theory ratio of true score variance over observed score variance. In this case, the observed scores are linear growth parameters (for example, β from technical note 3.1). We can compute the variances of these parameters directly from the data (see step 5). We must estimate the variance of the true scores under the assumption that the observed variance equals the true score variance plus the ratio of the error variance over the variance of the times of assessment.

$$\hat{\sigma}_\theta^2 = \sigma_\theta^2 + \frac{\hat{\sigma}_e^2}{M_{SST}}$$

To compute this, one needs an estimate of the error variance (which is computed in steps 1 and 2). One also needs an estimate of the variance of the times of assessment (which is computed in steps 3 and 4). It is important to note that when all times for assessment are the same for each student in the set, then SST (step 3) from a single student can be used in the denominator of the ratio as a substitute for M_{SST}.

However, when students have assessments at different times and in different numbers, then one must compute some central tendency of the individual *SST*s (see step 4).

Technical Note 4.2: Reliability of Curvilinear Growth Scores

The basic equation for reliability of curvilinear growth scores is:

$$\rho_{\hat{\theta}\,LN} = \frac{\hat{\sigma}^2_{\theta\,LN}}{\sigma^2_{\hat{\theta}\,LN}}$$

Elements important to the evaluation of the equation include:

θ_{LN} = growth parameter for an individual p when x and y are in natural log form

$\rho_{\hat{\theta}\,LN}$ = estimated reliability of the curvilinear growth parameter when x and y are in natural log form

$\hat{\sigma}^2_{\theta\,LN}$ = estimated variance of the true curvilinear growth parameter when x and y are in natural log form

$\sigma^2_{\hat{\theta}\,LN}$ = estimated variance of the observed growth parameter when x and y are in natural log form

$MSE_{p\,LN}$ = mean squared error for an individual p when x and y are in natural log form

y_{LN} = observed score in natural log form

$\hat{y}_{LN}$ = predicted score when x and y are in natural log form

$\hat{\sigma}^2_{e\,LN}$ = estimated measurement error variance when x and y are in natural log form

$SST_{p\,LN}$ = variance of assessment time for an individual p when x and y are in natural log form

$x_{i\,LN}$ = day in natural log form on which specific assessment was administered

$M_{SST\,LN}$ = estimated variance of observation times when x and y are in natural log form

m_{LN} = unstandardized slope for an individual p when x and y are in natural log form

N_p = number of individuals in the set (for example, class)

See figure A.5.

Compute:	
Step 1: Mean squared error of OLS regression for each individual p when x and y are in natural log form	$MSE_{p\,LN} = \dfrac{\Sigma(y_{LN} - \hat{y}_{LN})^2}{N_p - 2}$
Step 2: Estimated measurement error variance—average of $MSE_{p\,LN}$ from OLS regression for each individual p when x and y are in natural log form	$\hat{\sigma}^2_{e\,LN} = \dfrac{\Sigma MSE_{p\,LN}}{N_p}$

Step 3: Variance of assessment times for each individual p when x and y are in natural log form	$SST_{p\,LN} = \Sigma(x_{i\,LN} - \bar{x}_{i\,LN})^2$
Step 4: Estimated variance of assessment times— average of $SST_{p\,LN}$ for each individual p when x and y are in natural log form	$M_{SST\,LN} = \dfrac{\Sigma SST_{p\,LN}}{N_p}$
Step 5: Estimated observed growth parameter variance when x and y are in natural log form	$\sigma^2_{\hat{\theta}\,LN} = \dfrac{\Sigma(m_{LN} - \bar{m}_{LN})^2}{N_p - 1}$
Step 6: Estimated true growth parameter variance when x and y are in natural log form	$\hat{\sigma}^2_{\theta\,LN} = \sigma^2_{\hat{\theta}\,LN} - \dfrac{\hat{\sigma}^2_{e\,LN}}{M_{SST\,LN}}$
Step 7: Estimated reliability of growth parameter when x and y are in natural log form	$\rho_{\hat{\theta}\,LN} = \dfrac{\hat{\sigma}^2_{\theta\,LN}}{\sigma^2_{\hat{\theta}\,LN}}$
Report: $\rho_{\hat{\theta}\,LN}$	

Figure A.5: Computing the reliability of curvilinear growth scores.

As indicted by the basic equation, the reliability of the curvilinear growth scores (for example, slopes or growth parameters) follows the traditional classical test theory ratio of true score variance over observed score variance. This is the same for the reliability of the linear growth scores described in technical note 4.1. All assumptions I described for the reliability of the linear growth scores apply to the reliability of the curvilinear growth scores.

Technical Note 4.3: Reliability of Difference Scores

The basic equation for reliability of difference scores is:

$$\hat{p}(D) = \frac{\sigma^2_{yf}\,\hat{p}\,(y_f y_f) + \sigma^2_{yl}\,\hat{p}\,(y_l y_l) - 2\sigma_{yf}\,\sigma_{yl}p(y_f y_l)}{(\sigma^2_{yf}) + (\sigma^2_{yl}) - 2\sigma_{yf}\,\sigma_{yl}p(y_f y_l)}$$

Elements important to the evaluation of the equation include:

$\hat{p}(D)$ = estimated reliability of the difference scores

σ^2_{yf} = variance of the observed scores (y) for the first (f) assessment

$\hat{p}(y_f y_f)$ = estimated reliability of the observed scores for the first (f) assessment

σ^2_{yl} = variance of the observed scores (y) for the last (l) assessment

$\hat{p}(y_l y_l)$ = estimated reliability of the observed scores for the last (l) assessment

σ_{yf} = standard deviation of observed scores for the first (f) assessment

σ_{yl} = standard deviation of observed scores for the last (l) assessment

$p(y_f y_l)$ = correlation between the observed scores for the first (f) and last (l) assessments

N = number of students receiving observed scores on the first and last assessments

See figure A.6.

Compute:	
Step 1: Variance of observed scores for the first (f) assessment	$\sigma^2_{yf} = \dfrac{\Sigma(y_f - \bar{y}_f)}{N}$
Step 2: Standard deviation of the observed scores for the first (f) assessment	$\sigma_{yf} = \sqrt{\sigma^2_{yf}}$
Step 3: Variance of observed scores for the last (l) assessment	$\sigma^2_{yl} = \dfrac{\Sigma(y_l - \bar{y}_l)}{N}$
Step 4: Standard deviation of the observed scores for the last (l) assessment	$\sigma_{yl} = \sqrt{\sigma^2_{yl}}$
Step 5: Estimated reliability of the first (f) assessment $\hat{p}(y_f y_f)$	The estimated reliability of the first assessment should be computed using standard formulas (for example, coefficient alpha) or a reasoned estimate can be used (for example, 0.75).
Step 6: Estimated reliability of the last (l) assessment $\hat{p}(y_l y_l)$	The estimated reliability of the last assessment should be computed using standard formulas (for example, coefficient alpha) or a reasoned estimate can be used (for example, 0.75).
Step 7: Correlation between first and last scores $p(y_f y_l)$	$p(y_f y_l) = \dfrac{\Sigma y_f y_l - N\bar{y}_f \bar{y}_l}{\sqrt{\Sigma y_f^2 - N\bar{y}_f^2} \ \sqrt{\Sigma y_l^2 - N\bar{y}_l^2}}$
Step 8: Estimated reliability of difference scores $\hat{p}(D)$	$\hat{p}(D) = \dfrac{\sigma^2_{yf}\hat{p}(y_f y_f) + \sigma^2_{yl}\hat{p}(y_l y_l) - 2\sigma_{yf}\sigma_{yl}p(y_f y_l)}{(\sigma^2_{yf}) + (\sigma^2_{yl}) - 2\sigma_{yf}\sigma_{yl}p(y_f y_l)}$
Report: $\hat{p}(D)$	

Figure A.6: Computing the reliability of difference scores.

The reliability of the difference scores requires several elements not necessary for computing the reliabilities of linear or curvilinear growth scores. These are addressed in steps 1 through 7. One can easily compute all of these elements from the observed data except for the estimated reliabilities of the first and last assessments (steps 5 and 6, respectively). These can be computed using any standard formula, such as Cronbach's coefficient alpha. A computed reliability for first and last assessments will provide the most accurate estimate of the reliability of difference scores. However, if test data are not available to do so, then an estimate of the reliability of these assessments can be made and used for steps 5 and 6. Based on the research described in the introduction regarding the reliabilities of classroom assessments, a low estimate might be 0.50, and a high estimate might be 0.80.

References and Resources

Alonzo, A. C., & Steedle, J. T. (2009). Developing and assessing a force and motion learning progression. *Science Education*, *93*(3), 389–421.

American Educational Research Association, American Psychological Association, & National Council on Measurement in Education. (1999). *The standards for educational and psychological testing*. Washington, DC: American Educational Research Association.

American Educational Research Association, American Psychological Association, & National Council on Measurement in Education. (2014). *The standards for educational and psychological testing*. Washington, DC: American Educational Research Association.

Anderson, J. R. (1995). *Learning and memory: An integrated approach*. New York: Wiley.

Andrade, H. L. (2013). Classroom assessment in the context of learning theory and research. In J. H. McMillan (Ed.), *SAGE handbook of research on classroom assessment* (pp. 17–34). Los Angeles: SAGE.

Ayres, L. P. (1909). *Laggards in our schools: A study of retardation and elimination in city school systems*. New York: Charities Publication Committee.

Baker, B. O., Hardyck, C. D., & Petrinovich, L. F. (1966). Weak measurements vs. strong statistics: An empirical critique of S. S. Stevens' proscriptions on statistics. *Educational and Psychological Measurement*, *26*, 291–309.

Bays, T. (1764). *An essay toward solving a problem in the doctrine of chances*. Accessed at www.stat.ucla.edu/history/essay .pdf on June 12, 2017.

Belgrad, S. F. (2013). Portfolios and e-portfolios: Student reflection, self-assessment, and goal setting in the learning process. In J. H. McMillan (Ed.), *SAGE handbook of research on classroom assessment* (pp. 331–346). Los Angeles: SAGE.

Bereiter, C. (1963). Some persisting dilemmas in the measurement of change. In C. W. Harris (Ed.), *Problems in measuring change* (pp. 3–20). Madison: University of Wisconsin Press.

Black, P., & Wiliam, D. (1998a). Assessment and classroom learning. *Assessment in education: Principles, policy and practice*, *5*(1), 7–74.

Black, P., & Wiliam, D. (1998b). Inside the black box: Raising standards through classroom assessment. *Phi Delta Kappan*, *80*(2), 139–148.

Bonner, S. M. (2013). Validity in classroom assessment: Purposes, properties, and principles. In J. H. McMillan (Ed.), *SAGE handbook of research on classroom assessment* (pp. 87–106). Los Angeles: SAGE.

Brennan, R. L. (Ed.). (2006). *Educational measurement* (4th ed.). Washington, DC: American Council on Education and Praeger.

Briggs, D. C., Alonzo, A. C., Schwab, C., & Wilson, M. (2006). Diagnostic assessment with ordered multiple-choice items. *Educational Assessment, 11*(1), 33–63.

Briggs, D. C., Ruiz-Primo, M. A., Furtak, E., Shepard, L., & Yin, Y. (2012). Meta-analytic methodology and inferences about the efficacy of formative assessment. *Educational Measurement: Issues and Practice, 31*(4), 13–17.

Brookhart, S. M. (2013). Classroom assessment in the context of motivation theory and research. In J. H. McMillan (Ed.), *SAGE handbook of research on classroom assessment* (pp. 35–54). Los Angeles: SAGE.

Brown, G. T. L., & Harris, L. R. (2013). Student self-assessment. In J. H. McMillan (Ed.), *SAGE handbook of research on classroom assessment* (pp. 367–394). Los Angeles: SAGE.

Brown, W. (1910). Some experimental results in the correlation of mental abilities. *British Journal of Psychology, 3*(3), 296–322.

Brown, W. (1913). The effects of "observational errors" and other factors upon correlation coefficients in psychology. *British Journal of Psychology, 6*(2), 223–238.

Burke, C. J. (1953). Additive scales and statistics. *Psychological Review, 60*(1), 73–75.

Campbell, C. (2013). Research on teacher competency in classroom assessment. In J. H. McMillan (Ed.), *SAGE handbook of research on classroom assessment* (pp. 71–84). Los Angeles: SAGE.

Carifio, J., & Perla, R. J. (2007). Ten common misunderstandings, misconceptions, persistent myths and urban legends about Likert scales and Likert response formats and their antidotes. *Journal of Social Sciences, 3*(3), 106–116.

Chisholm, R. M. (1973). *The problem of the criterion.* Milwaukee: Marquette University Press.

Cohen, J. (1988). *Statistical power analysis for the behavioral sciences* (2nd ed.). Hillsdale, NJ: Erlbaum.

Collins, L. M., & Sayer, A. G. (Eds). (2001). *New methods for the analysis of change.* Washington, DC: American Psychological Association.

Conant, J. B. (1953). *Education and liberty: The role of the schools in a modern democracy.* Cambridge, MA: Harvard University Press.

Confrey, J., & Maloney, A. (2010, October). *Building formative assessments around learning trajectories as situated in the CCSS.* Paper presented at the fall meeting of the State Collaboratives on Assessment and Student Standards' Formative Assessment for Students and Teachers, Savannah, GA.

Cronbach, L. J. (1971). Test validation. In R. L. Thorndike (Ed.), *Educational measurement* (2nd ed., pp. 443–507). Washington, DC: American Council on Education.

Cronbach, L. J., & Meehl, P. E. (1955). Construct validity in psychological tests. *Psychological Bulletin, 52*(4), 281–302.

Cronbach, L. J., & Shavelson, R. J. (2004). My current thoughts on coefficient alpha and successor procedures. *Educational and Psychological Measurement, 64*(3), 391–418.

Cureton, E. E. (1958). The definition and estimation of test reliability. *Educational and Psychological Measurement, 18*(4), 715–738.

Durm, M. W. (1993). An A is not an A is not an A: A history of grading. *The Educational Forum, 57*(3), 294–297.

Duschl, R. A. (2006). Learning progressions as babushkas. *Measurement, 14*(1–2), 116–119.

Ebel, R. L. (1951). Estimation of the reliability of ratings. *Psychometrika, 16*(4), 407–424.

Engelhart, M. D., & Thomas, M. (1966). Rice as the inventor of the comparative test. *Journal of Educational Measurement, 3*(2), 141–145.

Feldt, L. S., & Brennan, R. L. (1993). Reliability. In R. L. Linn (Ed.), *Educational measurement* (3rd ed., pp. 105–146). Phoenix: Oryx Press.

Frisbie, D. A. (1988). Reliability of scores from teacher-made tests. *Educational Measurement: Issues and Practice, 7*(1), 25–35.

Frisbie, D. A. (2005). Measurement 101: Some fundamentals revisited. *Educational Measurement: Issues and Practice, 24*(3), 21–28.

Galton, F. (1888). Co-relations and their measurement, chiefly from anthropometric data. *Proceedings of the Royal Society of London, 45,* 135–145.

Garrett, H. E. (1937). *Statistics in psychology and education* (2nd ed.). New York: Longmans, Green.

Gill, B., Bruch, J., & Booker, K. (2013, September). *Using alternative student growth measures for evaluating teacher performance: What the literature says.* Washington, DC: U.S. Department of Education, Institute of Education Sciences, National Center for Education Evaluation and Regional Assistance, Regional Educational Laboratory Mid-Atlantic. Accessed at http://ies.ed.gov/ncee/edlabs/regions/midatlantic/pdf/REL_2013002.pdf on December 15, 2016.

Goodwin, L. D., & Leech, N. L. (2003). The meaning of validity in the new Standards for Educational and Psychological Testing: Implications for measurement courses. *Measurement and Evaluation in Counseling and Development, 36*(3), 181–191.

Guilford, J. P. (1946). New standards for test evaluation. *Educational and Psychological Measurement, 6*(4), 427–438.

Guilfoyle, C. (2006). NCLB: Is there life beyond testing? *Educational Leadership, 64*(3), 8–13.

Gulliksen, H. (1950). *Theory of mental tests.* New York: Wiley.

Guttman, L. (1945). A basis for analyzing test-retest reliability. *Psychometrika, 10*(4), 255–282.

Haertel, E. H. (2006). Reliability. In R. L. Brennan (Ed.), *Educational measurement* (4th ed., pp. 65–110). Washington, DC: American Council on Education and Praeger.

Hathcoat, J. D. (2013). Validity semantics in educational and psychological assessment. *Practical Assessment, Research and Evaluation, 18*(9), 1–14.

Hattie, J. (1984). An empirical study of various indices for determining unidimensionality. *Multivariate Behavioral Research, 19*(1), 49–78.

Hattie, J. (1985). Methodology review: Assessing unidimensionality of tests and items. *Applied Psychological Measurement, 9*(2), 139–164.

Hattie, J. (2009). *Visible learning: A synthesis of over 800 meta-analyses relating to achievement.* New York: Routledge.

Hattie, J. (2012). *Visible learning for teachers: Maximizing impact on learning.* New York: Routledge.

Hattie, J., Krakowski, K., Rogers, H. J., & Swaminathan, H. (1996). An assessment of Stout's index of essential unidimensionality. *Applied Psychological Measurement, 20*(1), 1–14.

Hays, W. L. (1973). *Statistics for the social sciences* (2nd ed.). New York: Holt, Rinehart and Winston.

Haystead, M. W. (2016, January). *An analysis of the relationship between English language arts and mathematics achievement and essential learning mastery in grades 3 and 4.* Bloomington, IN: Marzano Research. Accessed at www.marzanoresearch.com/technology/clark-pleasant-istep-ela-math-exec-summary on December 15, 2016.

Haystead, M. W., & Marzano, R. J. (2017). *The Marzano true score calculator.* Bloomington, IN: Marzano Research.

Heflebower, T., Hoegh, J. K., & Warrick, P. (2014). *A school leader's guide to standards-based grading.* Bloomington, IN: Marzano Research.

Heritage, M. (2013). Gathering evidence of student understanding. In J. H. McMillan (Ed.), *SAGE handbook of research on classroom assessment* (pp. 179–195). Los Angeles: SAGE.

Herman, J. L., & Choi, K. (2008, August). *Formative assessment and the improvement of middle school science learning: The role of teacher accuracy* (CRESST report No. 740). Los Angeles: University of California Graduate School of Education and Information Studies, National Center for Research on Evaluation, Standards, and Student Testing.

Hogan, T. P. (2013). Constructed-response approaches for classroom assessment. In J. H. McMillan (Ed.), *SAGE handbook of research on classroom assessment* (pp. 275–292). Los Angeles: SAGE.

Horst, P. (1966). *Psychological measurement and prediction.* Belmont, CA: Wadsworth.

Houts, P. L. (Ed.). (1977). *The myth of measurability.* New York: Hart.

Kamin, L. J. (1977). The politics of IQ. In P. L. Houts (Ed.), *The myth of measurability* (pp. 45–65). New York: Hart.

Kane, M. T. (1992). An argument-based approach to validity. *Psychological Bulletin, 112*(3), 527–535.

Kane, M. T. (2001). Current concerns in validity theory. *Journal of Educational Measurement, 38*(4), 319–342.

Kane, M. T. (2009). Validating the interpretations and uses of test scores. In R. W. Lissitz (Ed.), *The concept of validity: Revisions, new directions, and applications* (pp. 39–64). Charlotte, NC: Information Age.

Kane, M. T. (2011). The errors of our ways. *Journal of Educational Measurement, 48*(1), 12–30.

Kelley, T. L. (1942). The reliability coefficient. *Psychometrika, 7*(2), 75–83.

Kifer, E. (1994). Development of the Kentucky Instructional Results Information System (KIRIS). In T. R. Guskey (Ed.), *High stakes performance assessment: Perspectives on Kentucky's educational reform* (pp. 7–18). Thousand Oaks, CA: Corwin Press.

Kingston, N., & Nash, B. (2011). Formative assessment: A meta-analysis and a call for research. *Educational Measurement: Issues and Practice, 30*(4), 28–37.

Kinyua, K., & Okunya, L. O. (2014). Validity and reliability of teacher-made tests: Case study of year 11 in Nyahururu District of Kenya. *African Educational Research Journal, 2*(2), 61–71.

Kline, P. (1994). *An easy guide to factor analysis.* New York: Routledge.

Knapp, T. R. (1990). Treating ordinal scales as interval scales: An attempt to resolve the controversy. *Nursing Research, 39*(2), 121–123.

Lachlan-Haché, L., Cushing, E., & Bivona, L. (2012, November). *Student learning objectives: Benefits, challenges, and solutions.* Washington, DC: American Institutes for Research. Accessed at www.air.org/sites/default/files /downloads/report/Student-Learning-Objectives-Benefits-Challenges-Solutions.pdf on December 15, 2016.

Lane, S. (2013). Performance assessment. In J. H. McMillan (Ed.), *SAGE handbook of research on classroom assessment* (pp. 313–330). Los Angeles: SAGE.

Langford, D. P. (2015). *Tool time for education handbook* (Version 15). Molt, MT: Langford International.

Lindquist, E. F. (Ed.). (1951). *Educational measurement.* Washington, DC: American Council on Education.

Linn, R. L. (Ed.). (1993). *Educational measurement* (3rd ed.). Phoenix: Oryx Press.

Linn, R. L. (2001). A century of standardized testing: Controversies and pendulum swings. *Educational Assessment, 7*(1), 29–38.

Lord, F. M. (1959). Problems in mental test theory arising from errors of measurement. *Journal of the American Statistical Association, 54*(286), 472–479.

Lord, F. M., & Novick, M. R. (1968). *Statistical theories of mental test scores.* Reading, MA: Addison-Wesley.

Lubin, A. (1962). Statistics. *Annual Review of Psychology, 13*(1), 345–370.

Magnusson, D. (1967). *Test theory* (H. Mabon, Trans.). Reading, MA: Addison-Wesley.

Marzano, R. J. (1992). *A different kind of classroom: Teaching with dimensions of learning.* Alexandria, VA: Association for Supervision and Curriculum Development.

Marzano, R. J. (2000). *Transforming classroom grading.* Alexandria, VA: Association for Supervision and Curriculum Development.

Marzano, R. J. (2006). *Classroom assessment and grading that work.* Alexandria, VA: Association for Supervision and Curriculum Development.

Marzano, R. J. (2010). *Formative assessment and standards-based grading.* Bloomington, IN: Marzano Research.

Marzano, R. J. (2017). *The new art and science of teaching.* Bloomington, IN: Solution Tree Press & Association for Supervision and Curriculum Development.

Marzano, R. J., Basileo, L. D., & Toth, M. D. (2015, May). *Marzano Center student learning objectives.* West Palm Beach, FL: Learning Sciences International.

Marzano, R. J., & Haystead, M. W. (2008). *Making standards useful in the classroom.* Alexandria, VA: Association for Supervision and Curriculum Development.

Marzano, R. J., Heflebower, T., Hoegh, J. K., Warrick, P., & Grift, G. (2016). *Collaborative teams that transform schools: The next step in PLCs.* Bloomington, IN: Marzano Research.

Marzano, R. J., & Kendall, J. S. (1996). *A comprehensive guide to designing standards-based districts, schools, and classrooms.* Alexandria, VA: Association for Supervision and Curriculum Development.

Marzano, R. J., & Kendall, J. S. (2007). *The new taxonomy of educational objectives* (2nd ed.). Thousand Oaks, CA: Corwin Press.

Marzano, R. J., & Kendall, J. S. (2008). *Designing and assessing educational objectives: Applying the new taxonomy.* Thousand Oaks, CA: Corwin Press.

Marzano, R. J., Norford, J. S., Finn, M., & Finn, D., III. (2017). *A handbook for personalized competency-based education.* Bloomington, IN: Marzano Research.

Marzano, R. J., & Toth, M. D. (2013). *Teacher evaluation that makes a difference: A new model for teacher growth and student achievement.* Alexandria, VA: Association for Supervision and Curriculum Development.

Marzano, R. J., Yanoski, D. C., Hoegh, J. K., & Simms, J. A. (2013). *Using Common Core standards to enhance classroom instruction and assessment.* Bloomington, IN: Marzano Research.

Masters, G., & Forster, M. (1996). *Progress maps: Assessment resource kit.* Melbourne, Australia: Australian Council for Educational Research.

McKnight, C. C., Crosswhite, F. J., Dossey, J. A., Kifer, E., Swafford, J. O., Travers, K. J., et al. (1987). *The underachieving curriculum: Assessing U.S. school mathematics from an international perspective.* Champaign, IL: Stipes.

McMillan, J. H. (Ed.). (2013a). *SAGE handbook of research on classroom assessment.* Los Angeles: SAGE.

McMillan, J. H. (2013b). Why we need research on classroom assessment. In J. H. McMillan (Ed.), *SAGE handbook of research on classroom assessment* (pp. 3–16). Los Angeles: SAGE.

Messick, S. (1975). The standard problem: Meaning and values in measurement and evaluation. *American Psychologist, 30*(10), 955–966.

Messick, S. (1993). Validity. In R. L. Linn (Ed.), *Educational measurement* (3rd ed., pp. 13–104). Phoenix: Oryx Press.

National Commission on Excellence in Education. (1983). *A nation at risk: The imperative for educational reform.* Washington, DC: U.S. Government Printing Office.

National Council of Teachers of Mathematics. (1989). *Curriculum and evaluation standards for school mathematics.* Reston, VA: Author.

National Education Goals Panel. (1991, January). *The National Education Goals report: Building a nation of learners.* Washington, DC: Author.

National Education Goals Panel. (1993, November). *Promises to keep: Creating high standards for American students* (Technical Report No. 94-01). Washington, DC: Author.

National Governors Association Center for Best Practices & Council of Chief State School Officers. (2010a). *Common Core State Standards for English language arts and literacy in history/social studies, science, and technical subjects.* Washington, DC: Authors. Accessed at www.corestandards.org/assets/CCSSI_ELA%20Standards.pdf on December 15, 2016.

National Governors Association Center for Best Practices & Council of Chief State School Officers. (2010b). *Common Core State Standards for mathematics.* Washington, DC: Authors. Accessed at www.corestandards.org/assets/CCSSI_Math%20Standards.pdf on December 15, 2016.

National Research Council. (2007). *Taking science to school: Learning and teaching science in grades K–8.* Washington, DC: National Academies Press.

NGSS Lead States. (2013). *Next Generation Science Standards: For states, by states.* Washington, DC: National Academies Press.

Parkes, J. (2013). Reliability in classroom assessment. In J. H. McMillan (Ed.), *SAGE handbook of research on classroom assessment* (pp. 107–123). Los Angeles: SAGE.

Pearson, K. (1920). Notes on the history of correlation. *Biometrika, 13*(1), 25–45.

Phelps, R. P. (Ed.). (2009). *Correcting fallacies about educational and psychological testing.* Washington, DC: American Psychological Association.

Plake, B. S., Hambleton, R. K., & Jaeger, R. M. (1995). *A new standard-setting method for performance assessments: The dominant profile judgment method and some field-test results.* Paper presented at the annual meeting of the American Educational Research Association, San Francisco.

Popham, W. J. (2006). Phony formative assessments: Buyer beware! *Educational Leadership, 64*(3), 86–87.

Popham, W. J. (2017). *Classroom assessment: What teachers need to know* (8th ed.). Boston: Pearson.

Prince, C. D., Schuermann, P. J., Guthrie, J. W., Witham, P. J., Milanowski, A. T., & Thorn, C. A. (2009, August). *The other 69 percent: Fairly rewarding the performance of teachers of nontested subjects and grades.* Washington, DC: Center for Educator Compensation Reform.

Randel, B., & Clark, T. (2013). Measuring classroom assessment practices. In J. H. McMillan (Ed.), *SAGE handbook of research on classroom assessment* (pp. 145–164). Los Angeles: SAGE.

Reckase, M. D. (1995). Portfolio assessment: A theoretical estimate of score reliability. *Educational Measurement: Issues and Practice, 14*(1), 12–14, 31.

Rodriguez, M. C., & Haladyna, T. M. (2013). Writing selected-response items for classroom assessment. In J. H. McMillan (Ed.), *SAGE handbook of research on classroom assessment* (pp. 293–312). Los Angeles: SAGE.

Rogosa, D., Brandt, D., & Zimowski, M. (1982). A growth curve approach to the measurement of change. *Psychological Bulletin, 92*(3), 726–748.

Rothman, R. (2011). *Something in common: The Common Core standards and the next chapter in American education.* Cambridge, MA: Harvard Education Press.

Salkind, N. J. (2017). *Statistics for people who (think they) hate statistics: Using Excel 2016* (4th ed.). Los Angeles: SAGE.

Schlosser, E., & Wilson, C. (2006). *Chew on this: Everything you don't want to know about fast food.* Boston: Houghton Mifflin.

Schmidt, W. H., McKnight, C. C., Cogan, L. S., Jakwerth, P. M., & Houang, R. T. (1998). *Facing the consequences: Using TIMSS for a closer look at U.S. mathematics and science education.* Dordrecht, the Netherlands: Kluwer.

Schneider, M. C., Egan, K. L., & Julian, M. W. (2013). Classroom assessment in the context of high-stakes testing. In J. H. McMillan (Ed.), *SAGE handbook of research on classroom assessment* (pp. 55–84). Los Angeles: SAGE.

Senders, V. L. (1953). A comment on Burke's additive scales and statistics. *Psychological Review, 60*(6), 423–424.

Shepard, L. A. (2008). A brief history of accountability testing, 1965–2007. In K. E. Ryan & L. A. Shepard (Eds.), *The future of test-based educational accountability* (pp. 25–46). New York: Routledge.

Simms, J. A. (2016, August). *The critical concepts.* Bloomington, IN: Marzano Research. Accessed at www.marzanoresearch.com/technology/the-critical-concepts on December 15, 2016.

Smith, C. L., Wiser, M., Anderson, C. W., & Krajcik, J. (2006). Implications of research on children's learning for standards and assessment: A proposed learning progression for matter and the atomic-molecular theory. *Measurement, 4*(1–2), 1–98.

Snider, T. Z. (2014, December 29). *Let kids sleep later.* Accessed at www.cnn.com/2014/08/28/opinion/snider-school-later-start-times on December 19, 2016.

Songer, N. B., Kelcey, B., & Gotwals, A. W. (2009). How and when does complex reasoning occur?: Empirically driven development of a learning progression focused on complex reasoning about biodiversity. *Journal of Research in Science Teaching, 46*(6), 610–631.

Spearman, C. (1904). The proof and measurement of association between two things. *American Journal of Psychology, 15*(1), 72–101.

Spearman, C. (1910). Correlation calculated from faulty data. *British Journal of Psychology, 3*(3), 271–295.

Stevens, S. S. (1946). On the theory of scales of measurement. *Science, 103*(2684), 677–680.

Stevens, S. S. (Ed.). (1951). *Handbook of experimental psychology.* New York: Wiley.

Stevens, S. S. (1959). Measurement, psychophysics and utility. In C. W. Churchman & P. Ratoosh (Eds.), *Measurement: Definitions and theories.* New York: Wiley.

Stevens, S. S. (1960). The predicament in design and significance. *Contemporary Psychology, 5*, 273–276.

Terman, L. M. (1916). *The measurement of intelligence.* Boston: Houghton Mifflin.

The New York Times. (2014, October 21). Taking sports out of school. Accessed at www.nytimes.com/roomfordebate /2014/10/21/taking-sports-out-of-school-2 on December 19, 2016.

Thissen, D., & Wainer, H. (Eds.). (2001). *Test scoring.* Mahwah, NJ: Erlbaum.

Thorndike, E. L. (1904). *An introduction to the theory of mental and social measurements.* New York: Science Press.

Thorndike, R. L. (Ed.). (1971). *Educational measurement* (2nd ed.). Washington, DC: American Council on Education.

Tomlinson, C. A., & Moon, T. R. (2013). Differentiation and classroom assessment. In J. H. McMillan (Ed.), *SAGE handbook of research on classroom assessment* (pp. 415–430). Los Angeles: SAGE.

Traub, R. E. (1997). Classical test theory in historical perspective. *Educational Measurement: Issues and Practice, 16*(4), 8–14.

U.S. Department of Education. (2010, March). *A blueprint for reform: The reauthorization of the Elementary and Secondary Education Act.* Washington, DC: Author.

Valencia, S. W., Stallman, A. C., Commeyras, M., Pearson, P. D., & Hartman, D. K. (1991). Four measures of topical knowledge: A study of construct validity. *Reading Research Quarterly, 26*(3), 204–233.

Wiliam, D. (2016). *Leadership for teacher learning: Creating a culture where all teachers improve so that all students succeed.* West Palm Beach, FL: Learning Sciences International.

Willett, J. B. (1985). *Investigating systematic individual difference in academic growth* (Unpublished doctoral dissertation). Stanford University, Palo Alto, CA.

Willett, J. B. (1988). Questions and answers in the measurement of change. *Review of Research in Education, 15,* 345–422.

Yerkes, R. M. (Ed.). (1921). *Memoirs of the National Academy of Sciences: Psychological examining in the United States Army* (Vol. 15). Washington, DC: U.S. Government Printing Office.

Index

A

accountability movement, 3
accuracy, 8
alternative-choice items, 40
American Educational Research Association (AERA), 1, 48, 50
American Psychological Association (APA), 1, 48, 50
Anderson, J., 67
Andrade, H., 25–26, 105, 106
argument-based perspective, 17, 20–21
Army Alpha test, 5
assessments
    See also classroom assessment (CA); large-scale assessments; parallel assessments
    defined, 35, 36
    formative, 72–73
    interim (benchmark), 6
    self-assessments, student, 52–55
    student-generated, 56
    summative, 72–73
    year-end, 6–7
averages, weighted and unweighted, 99–102
average trend line, 67–68, 114–115
Ayres, L. P., 3

B

Belgrad, S., 51
benchmark (interim) assessments, 6
Bereiter, C., 30
best fit model, 68–70
Binet, A., 5
Bivona, L., 107

Black, P., 72
Blueprint for Reform, A (U.S, Department of Education), 106
Booker, K., 107
Brennan, R., 10, 64
Brookhart, S., 6
Bruch, J., 107

C

Campbell, C., 7
"Century of Standardized Testing: Controversies and Pendulum Swings, A" (Linn), 2
Chisholm, R., 18
Choi, K., 26
Clark, T., 6
classical test theory, 60, 83
classroom assessment (CA)
    See also reliability, classroom assessment paradigm for; validity, classroom assessment paradigm for
    concerns about, 7
    lack of research on, 1
    new paradigms, need for, 8
    role of, 6–7
Classroom Assessment and Grading That Work (Marzano), 24, 103
Classroom Assessment: What Teachers Need to Know (Popham), 1
Common Core State Standards (CCSS), 4, 21, 22, 26
compensatory approach, 102–103
completion items, 40
Conant, J., 3
conceptual equation for an individual score, 10, 63–64

confidence intervals, 11, 110–111
conjunctive approach, 102–104
construct validity, 17, 18, 19, 20
content validity, 17, 18, 19, 20, 21
correlation and reliability coefficients, 61–63
Council of Chief State School Officers (CCSSO), 4
covariance, 24
criterion measure, 18–19
criterion-related validity, 17, 18, 19, 20, 32–33
Cronbach, L., 9, 19, 64
Cronbach coefficient alpha formula, 64, 122
Cureton, E., 62
curvilinear growth scores, 86–99, 107–108, 120–121
curvilinear trend line, 67, 112–114
Cushing, E., 107
cut score, 36

D

decision making, 49
definitional investigation, 50
demonstrations, 50
difference (gain) score, 88–91, 107–108, 121–122
differentiated assessments, 58
dimensionality, 22–24
discussions, probing, 51–52
Duncan, A., 106

E

Ebel, R., 62
Edgeworth, F. Y., 61

Educational Measurement (Lindquist, Linn, Thorndike), 1
effect size, 52
Egan, K., 6–7, 21
Elementary and Secondary Education Act (ESEA), 3
elements, 13
error score, concept of, 60–61
essays, 47–48
Excel, 65, 70
excellence movement, 3
experimental inquiry, 49

F
factor analysis, 19
Feldt, L., 10, 64
fill-in-the-blank items, 40, 41
Finn, D., III, 27–28, 52, 103
Finn, M., 27–28, 52, 103
Formative Assessment and Standards-Based Grading (Marzano), 73, 103
formative assessments/scores, 72–73
format-specific scores, 37
Frisbie, D., 10, 18

G
gain (difference) score, 88–90, 107–108, 21–122
Galileo, 60
Garrett, H., 17
Gauss, C. F., 61
generalizability, 60
Gill, B., 107
growth scores
    curvilinear, 86–99, 107–108, 120–121
    difference (gain), 88–91, 107–108, 121–122
    linear, 84–86, 107–108, 118–120
    reconciling reliability estimates, 90–91, 107–108
    technology to calculate, 91–92
Gulliksen, H., 34, 61
Guttman, L., 63

H
Haladyna, T., 41
Hathcoat, J., 17, 18–19
Hattie, J., 52, 106
Hays, W., 115
Haystead, M. W., 65, 91

Heflebower, T., 22, 104
Heritage, M., 26
Herman, J., 26
historical investigation, 49
Hoegh, J., 13, 22, 104
Hogan, T., 42, 43, 47
Horst, P., 34

I
instructional feedback, 73–74
instrumental perspective, 17, 18–19, 20–21
intelligence tests, 5
interim (benchmark) assessments, 6
interval scale, 77
item response theory, 60

J
Journal of Educational Measurement, 1
Julian, M., 6–7, 21

K
Kahoot!, 55
Kamin, L., 5
Kane, M., 20, 21, 34, 37
Kelley, T., 61
KR20 and KR21 formulas, 64

L
Lachlan-Haché, L., 107
Laggards in Our Schools: A Study of Retardation and Elimination in City School Systems (Ayres), 3
Lane, S., 48
Langford, D. P., 52
large-scale assessments
    history of, 2–5
    paradigm for reliability, 8–11, 59–64
    paradigm for validity, 13, 39–46
learning progressions, 25–28
Lindquist, E. F., 1
linear growth parameter, 84
linear growth scores, 84–86, 107–108, 118–120
linear trend line, 66, 111–112
Linn, R. L., 1, 2
Lord, F., 22, 34–35

M
Magnusson, D., 34, 62
Mann, H., 2–3

Marzano, R. J., 13, 22, 24, 27–28, 48–50, 52, 65, 73, 91, 103, 106–107
matching items, 40
mathematical models
    average trend line, 67–68, 114–115
    curvilinear trend line, 67, 112–114
    linear trend line, 66, 111–112
    technology for, 70–72, 91–92
McMillan, J., 1, 6
measurement, defined, 34–35
"Measurement 101: Some Fundamentals Revisited" (Frisbie), 18
measurement process, 34–37, 56, 57
measurement scales, 76–79
measurement topics, 25
    residual, 104
    supplemental, 104–105
median, 102
Meehl, P., 19
Memoirs of the National Academy of Sciences: Psychological Examining in the United States Army (Yerkes), 5
Messick, S., 17, 20
mode, 102
Moon, T., 58
mounting evidence, method of, 74–76, 115–118
multiple-choice items, 40
multiple-response items, 41

N
National Academy of Sciences, 5
National Assessment of Educational Progress (NAEP), 3
National Commission on Excellence in Education, 3
National Council on Measurement in Education (NCME), 1, 48, 50
National Education Goals Panel, 21
National Governors Association Center for Best Practices, 4
National Research Council (NRC), 25
Nation at Risk, A (National Commission on Excellence in Education), 3
Next Generation Science Standards (NGSS), 21, 26
No Child Left Behind (NCLB), 4
nominal scale, 77
Norford, J., 27–28, 52, 103
Novick, M., 34–35

O

Obama, B., 106
observations, 55–56
observed score, 10, 12, 60, 84
"On the Theory of Scales of Measurement:
    (Stevens), 77
ordinal scale, 77
Otis, A., 5

P

parallel assessments
    defined, 14, 33
    structure of, 33–34
parallel assessments, designing and scoring
    assessments that cover one level of a
        proficiency scale, 55–56
    differentiated assessments, 58
    discussions, probing, 51–52
    essays, 47–48
    measurement process, 56, 57
    performance tasks, demonstrations,
        and presentations, 48–50
    planning, 56–58
    portfolios, 50–51
    self-assessments, student, 52–55
    traditional tests, 39–46
Parkes, J., 8, 22, 35, 60
Partnership for Assessment of Readiness
    for College and Careers (PARCC), 4
percentage scores, 44–45
performance assessments/tasks, 48–50
personal tracking matrix, 52–55
Popham, W. J., 1
portfolios, 50–51
precision, use of term, 59, 65, 83–84
presentations, 50
Prince, C., 107
probing discussions, 51–52
problem solving, 49
proficiency scales, 25
    assessments that cover one level of a,
        55–56
    inherently ordinal, 79–80
    internally consistent, 80–81
    issues regarding, 76–81
    scores, 43–46
    strong statistics theory, 81
    structure of, 28–32, 34
projective investigation, 49

psychometricians, 10

Q

Quizzizz, 55

R

Race to the Top (RTT), 106
Randel, B., 6
random measurement error, 10
random score, 61
ratio scale, 77
reliability
    classical test theory, 60
    coefficient, 10–11, 61–63, 64
    conceptual equation for an individual
        score, 10, 63–64
    confidence intervals, 11
    correlation and reliability coefficients,
        61–63, 64
    curvilinear growth scores, 86–99,
        107–108, 120–121
    curvilinear slope, 87–88, 90–91
    defined, 7, 8, 59, 83
    difference (gain) scores, 88–91, 107–
        108, 121–122
    error score, concept of, 60–61
    large-scale (traditional) assessment
        paradigm for, 8–11, 59–64
    linear growth scores, 84–86, 107–108,
        118–120
    observed score, 10, 12, 60
    random measurement error, 10
    of a set of slopes (linear slope), 85,
        90–91
    time-based equation, 12–13
    true score, concept of, 61
reliability, classroom assessment paradigm
    for
    average trend line, 67–68, 114–115
    best fit model, 68–70
    curvilinear trend line, 67, 112–114
    description of, 11–13
    linear trend line, 66, 111–112
    reconciliation model, 68
    technology, use of, 70–72, 91–92
report cards
    allowing students to increase their
        scores, 105–106
    conjunctive approach, 102–104
    median and mode, 102

supplemental measurement topics,
    104–105
    transforming, 93–106
    weighted and unweighted averages,
        99–102
residual measurement topics, 104
response codes, 45–46
Rice, J. M., 2, 78
Rodriguez, M., 41

S

SAGE Handbook of Research on Classroom
    Assessment, 1, 2
scale, defined, 35, 36
Schneider, M. C., 6–7, 21
school's (district) role in criterion-related
    validity, 32–33
scores
    See also growth scores
    cut, 36
    defined, 35, 36
    error, 60–61
    observed, 10, 12, 60, 84
    random, 61
    true, 61, 65–70
    universe, 60
scoring
    aberrant patterns, addressing, 46
    compensatory approach, 102–103
    conjunctive approach, 102–104
    median and mode, 102
    select-response items, 43–46
    short constructed-response items,
        43–46
    using percentage, 44–45
    using response codes, 45–46
    weighted and unweighted averages,
        99–102
scoring rubrics, 27–28
select-response items
    designing, 40–42
    scoring, 43–46
self-assessments, student, 52–55
self-regulated learning, 105–106
Senders, V., 79–80
Shavelson, R., 9
Shepard, L., 2–3, 4
short constructed-response items
    designing, 42–43
    scoring, 43–46

Simms, J., 13, 22, 24, 25

slope, trend line, 84

Smarter Balanced Assessment Consortium (SBAC), 4

Socrative, 55

Spearman, C., 61

Spearman-Brown formula, 64

standard error of measurement (SEM), 110–111

standards

as the basis of classroom assessment, 21–22

development of, 3–4

movement, 21

problem with, 21–22

Standards for Educational and Psychological Testing, The (AERA, APA, and NCME), 1, 48, 50

Stanford-Binet test, 5

Stevens, S. S., 34, 77

strong statistics theory, 81

student-generated assessments, 56

student learning objectives, 107

student   self-assessments, 52–55

summative assessments/scores, 72–73

supplemental measurement topics, 104–105

T

Taking Science to School (NRC), 25

teacher evaluations, transforming, 106–107

technology

to calculate reliability of growth scores, 91–92

for mathematical models, 70–72

test

defined, 35, 36

select-response items, designing, 40–42

select-response items, scoring, 43–46

short constructed-response items, designing, 42–43

short constructed-response items, scoring, 43–46

traditional, designing and scoring, 39–46

use of term, 39

Thissen, D., 22–23

Thorndike, E., 77–78

Thorndike, R. L., 1

Tomlinson, C. A., 58

Toth, M. D., 106–107

Traub, R., 60, 61

Treman, L., 5

true-false items, 41

true score, concept of, 61, 65–70

U

unidimensionality, 22

U.S. Department of Education, 106

universe score, 60

unweighted averages, 99–102

V

Valencia, S., 51

validity

argument-based perspective, 17, 20–21

construct, 17, 18, 19, 20

content, 17, 18, 19, 20, 21

criterion-related, 17, 18, 19, 20, 32–33

defined, 7, 13, 17

instrumental perspective, 17, 18–19, 20–21

large-scale (traditional) assessment paradigm for, 13, 39–46

types of, 17

validity, classroom assessment paradigm for

argument-based perspective, 20–21

construct validity, 20

content validity, 20, 21

criterion-related validity, 20, 32–33

description of, 14–15

dimensionality, 22–24

instrumental perspective, 20–21

measurement process, 34–37

measurement topics, 25

parallel assessments, 33–34

proficiency scales, 25, 28–32, 34

standards as the basis of, 21–22

value-added measures (VAMs), 106–107

variance, 63

Visible Learning (Hattie), 52

Visible Learning for Teachers (Hattie), 52

voting techniques, 55

W

Wainer, H., 22–23

Warrick, P., 22, 104

weak measurement theory, 77, 79–81

weighted and unweighted averages, 99–102

Wiliam, D., 72, 73

Y

Yanoski, D., 13, 22

year-end assessments, 6–7

Yerkes, R. M., 5

Formative Assessment & Standards-Based Grading
Robert J. Marzano

Learn everything you need to know to implement an integrated system of assessment and grading. The author details the specific benefits of formative assessment and explains how to design and interpret three different types of formative assessments, how to track student progress, and how to assign meaningful grades. Detailed examples bring each concept to life, and chapter exercises reinforce the content.
BKL003

The New Art and Science of Teaching
Robert J. Marzano

This title is a greatly expanded volume of the original *The Art and Science of Teaching*, offering a framework for substantive change based on Robert J. Marzano's fifty years of education research. While the previous model focused on teacher outcomes, the new version places focus on student outcomes. Throughout the book, Dr. Marzano details the elements of three overarching categories of teaching, which define what must happen to optimize student learning.
BKF776

Essential Assessment
Cassandra Erkens, Tom Schimmer, and Nicole Dimich Vagle

Discover how to use the power of assessment to instill hope, efficacy, and achievement in your students. With this research-based resource, you'll explore six essential tenets of assessment—assessment purpose, communication of assessment results, accurate interpretation, assessment architecture, instructional agility, and student investment—that will help deepen your understanding of assessment to not only meet standards but also enhance students' academic success and self-fulfillment.
BKF752

Simplifying Common Assessment
Kim Bailey and Chris Jakicic

Built on the process featured in *Common Formative Assessment: A Toolkit for PLCs at Work™*, this book demonstrates how educators can develop effective and efficient assessments. The authors simplify assessment development to give teacher teams the confidence to write and use team-designed common formative assessments that help ensure all students master essential skills and concepts.
BKF750

The Assessment Toolkit

Transform your assessment practice into a powerful tool that inspires student learning. Find tips on how to involve students in the assessment process, integrate assessments into instruction, and ensure reporting practices that accurately measure student achievement. Help your team begin to build its own repertoire of assessments and make inferences about a student's ability to meet standards and curriculum goals.
KTF132

a division of

Solution Tree | Press

Solution Tree

Visit SolutionTree.com or call 800.733.6786 to order.

"Excellent engagement in what truly matters in **assessment**.

Great examples!"

—Carol Johnson, superintendent,
Central Dauphin School District, Pennsylvania

 PD Services

Our experts draw from decades of research and their own experiences to bring you practical strategies for designing and implementing quality assessments. You can choose from a range of customizable services, from a one-day overview to a multiyear process.

Book your assessment PD today!
888.763.9045

Solution Tree